THE "SHOWN" SERIES
EDITED BY LOUEY CHISHOLM

TREES

PLATE I

THE OAK

1. Oak Tree   2. Leaf Spray   3. Spray with Flower Catkins
4. Stamen Catkin   5. Seed Catkin   6. Fruit

TREES

BY

JANET HARVEY KELMAN

DESCRIBED BY

C. E. SMITH

THIRTY-TWO COLOURED PICTURES

THOMAS NELSON AND SONS, Ltd.
(Incorporating T. C. & E. C. JACK, Ltd.)
LONDON, EDINBURGH, NEW YORK
TORONTO, AND PARIS

To

THOMAS FORBES SACKVILLE WILSON

IN this little book I have written about some of the trees which you are likely to find growing wild in this country, and Miss Kelman has painted for you pictures of these trees, with drawings of the leaves and flowers and fruit, so that it will be easy for you to tell the name of each tree. But I think there is one question which you are sure to ask after reading this small book, and that is, "How do the trees grow?"

The tree grows very much as we do, by taking food and by breathing. The food of the tree is obtained from two sources: from the earth and from the air. Deep down in the earth lie the tree roots, and these roots suck up water from the soil in which they are embedded. This water, in which there is much nourishment, rises through many tiny cells in the woody stem till it reaches the leaf, twigs, and green leaves. As it rises the growing cells keep what they need of the water. The rest is given off as vapour by the leaves through many tiny pores, which you will not be able to see without a microscope.

While it is day the green leaves select from

the air a gas called carbonic acid gas. This they separate into two parts called oxygen and carbon. The plant does not need the oxygen as food, so the leaves return it to the air, but they keep the carbon. This carbon becomes mixed in some strange way with the water food drawn from the soil by the roots. Forming a liquid, it finds its way through many small cells and channels to feed the growing leaves and twigs and branches.

But, like ourselves, a tree if it is to live and thrive must breathe as well as take food. By night as well as by day the tree requires air for breathing. Scattered over the surface of the leaves, and indeed over the skin of the tree, are many tiny mouths or openings called stomata. It is by these that the tree breathes. It now takes from the air some oxygen, which, you will remember, is the gas that the leaves do not need in making their share of the tree food. Now you can see why it is that a tree cannot thrive if it is planted in a dusty, sooty town. The tiny mouths with which it breathes get filled up, and the tree is half-choked for lack of air. Also the pores of the leaves become clogged, so that the water which is not needed cannot easily escape from them. A heavy shower of rain is a welcome friend to our dusty town trees.

As a rule tree flowers are not so noticeable as those which grow in the woods and meadows.

Often the ring of gaily-coloured petals which form the corolla is awanting, so are the green or coloured sepals of the calyx, and the flower may consist, as in the Ash tree, of a small seed-vessel standing between two stamens, which have plenty of pollen dust in their fat heads.

It is very interesting to notice the various ways in which the tree flowers grow. In some trees the stamens and seed-vessels will be found close together, as in the Ash tree and Elm. Or they may grow on the same branch of a tree; but all the stamens will be grouped together on one stalk and all the seed-vessels close beside it on another stalk, as in the Oak tree. Or the stamen flowers may all be found on one tree without any seed flowers, and on another tree, some-times a considerable distance away, there will be found nothing but seed flowers. This occurs in the White Poplar or Abele tree.

You must never forget that both kinds of flowers are required if the tree is to produce new seed, and many books have been written to point out the wonderful ways in which the wind and the birds and the bees carry the stamen dust to the seed-vessels, which are waiting to receive it.

Each summer the tree adds a layer of new wood in a circle round the tree trunk; a broad circle when there has been sunshine and the tree has thriven well, and a narrow circle when the season has been wet and sunless. This new layer of wood is always found just under the bark or coarse, outer skin of the tree. The bark protects the soft young wood, and if it is eaten by cattle, or cut off by mischievous boys, then the layer of young wood is exposed, and the tree will die.

When winter approaches and the trees get ready for their long sleep, the cells in this layer of new wood slowly dry, and it becomes a ring of hard wood. If you look at a tree which has just been cut down, you will be able to tell how many years old the tree is by counting the circles of wood in the tree trunk. When a tree grows very slowly these rings are close and firm, and the wood of the tree is hard and valuable.

Many, many years ago, when a rich Scotch landlord lay dying, he said to his only son, "Jock, when you have nothing else to do, be sticking in a tree; it will aye be growing when you are sleeping." He was a clever, far-seeing old man, Jock's father, for he knew that in course of time trees grow to be worth money, and that to plant a tree was a sure and easy way of adding a little more to the wealth he loved so dearly.

But a tree has another and a greater value to us and to the world than the price which a wood merchant will give for it as timber. Think what a dear familiar friend the tree has been in the life of man! How different many of our best-loved tales would be without the trees that played so large a part in the lives of our favourite heroes. Where could Robin Hood and his merry men have lived and hunted but under the greenwood tree? Without the forest of Arden what refuge would have sheltered the mischief-loving Rosalind and her banished father? How often do we think of the stately Oak and Linden trees into which good old Baucis and Philemon were changed by the kindly gods.

And do you remember what secrets the trees told us as we lay under their shady branches on the hot midsummer days, while the leaves danced and flickered against the blue, blue sky? Can you tell what was the charm that held us like a dream in the falling dusk as we watched their heavy masses grow dark and gloomy against the silvery twilight sky?

In a corner of a Cumberland farmyard there grew a noble tree whose roots struck deep into the soil, and whose heavy branches shadowed much of the ground. "Why do you not cut it down?" asked a stranger; "it seems so much in the way." "Cut it down!" the farmer answered passionately. "I would sooner fall on my knees and worship it." To him the tree had spoken of a secret unguessed by Jock's father and by many other people who look at the trees with eyes that cannot see. He had learned that the mystery of tree life is one with the mystery

that underlies our own; that we share this
mystery with the sea, and the sun, and the
stars, and that by this mystery of life the whole
world is "bound with gold chains" of love "about
the feet of God."

C. E. SMITH.

LIST OF PLATES

xiii

TREES

PLATE I

THE OAK

OF all our forest trees the Oak is undoubtedly
the king. It is our most important tree, the
monarch of our woods, full of noble dignity and
grandeur in the summer sunshine, strong to en-
dure the buffeting of the wintry gales. It lives
to the great age of seven hundred years or more,
and is a true father of the forest. We read of the
Oak tree in the story books of long ago. There
are many Oak trees mentioned in the Bible. In
Greece the Oak was believed to be the first tree
that God created, and there grew a grove of
sacred Oaks which were said to utter prophecies.
The wood used for the building of the good ship
Argo was cut from this grove, and in times of
danger the planks of the ship spoke in warning
voices to the sailors.

In Rome a crown of Oak leaves was given to him
who should save the life of a citizen, and in this
country, in the days of the Druids, there were

A

many strange customs connected with the Oak
and its beautiful guest the mistletoe. The burning
of the Yule log of Oak is an ancient custom which
we trace to Druid times. It was lit by the priests
from the sacred altar, then the fires in all the
houses were put out, and the people relit them
with torches kindled at the sacred log. Even
now in remote parts of Yorkshire and Devonshire
the Yule log is brought in at Christmas-time
and half burned, then it is taken off the fire and
carefully laid aside till the following year.

We know that in Saxon times this country
was covered with dense forests, many of which
were of Oak trees. Huge herds of swine fed
on the acorns which lay in abundance under the
trees; and a man, when he wished to sell his piece
of forest, did not tell the buyer how much money
the wood in it was worth, but how many pigs
it could fatten. In times of famine the acorns
used to be ground, and bread was made of the
meal. There have been many famous Oak trees
in England: one of these we have all heard of—
the huge Oak at Boscobel in which King Charles
II. hid with a great many of his men after he
was defeated at the battle of Worcester.

I think you will have no difficulty in recognising
an Oak tree (1) at any time of the year. Look at
its trunk in winter: how dark and rough it is;
how wide and spreading at the bottom to give
its many roots a broad grip of the earth into which

they pierce deeply. Then as the stem rises it becomes narrower, as if the tree had a waist, for it broadens again as it reaches a height where the branches divide from the main trunk. And what huge branches these are—great rough, dark arms with many crooked knots or elbows, which shipbuilders prize for their trade. These Oak-tree arms are so large and heavy that the tree would need to be well rooted in the ground to stand firm when the gale is tossing its branches as if they were willow rods.

The Oak tree does not grow to a great height. It is a broad, sturdy tree, and it grows very slowly, so slowly that after it is grown up it rarely increases more than an inch in a year, and sometimes not even that. But just because the Oak tree lives so leisurely, it outlasts all its companions in the forest except, perhaps, the yew tree, and its beautiful hard, close-grained wood is the most prized of all our timber.

In the end of April or early in May, the Oak leaves (2) appear; very soft and tender they are too at first, and of a pale reddish green colour. But soon they darken in the sunshine and become a dark glossy green. Each leaf is feather-shaped and has a stalk. The margin is deeply waved into blunt lobes or fingers, and there is a strongly marked vein up the centre of the leaf, with slender veins running from it to the edge.

In autumn these leaves change colour: they

become a pale brown, and will hang for weeks
rustling in the branches till the young buds which
are to appear next year begin to form and so push
the old leaves off. If a shrivelling frost or a
blighting insect destroys all the young Oak leaves,
as sometimes happens, then the sturdy tree will
reclothe itself in a new dress of leaves, which
neither the Beech, nor the Chestnut, nor the
Maple, could do. It shows what a great deal of
life there is in the stout tree.

The flowers of the Oak arrive about the same
time as the leaves, and they grow in catkins
which are of two kinds. You will find a slender
hanging catkin (3) on which grow small bunches of
yellow-headed stamens (4). Among the stamens
you can see six or eight narrow sepals, but these
stamens have no scales to protect them as the
Hazel and Birch catkins have. On the same
branch grows a stouter, upright catkin, and on it
are one or maybe two or three tiny cups (5), made
of soft green leaves called bracts, and in the centre
of this cup sits the seed-vessel, crowned with
three blunt points. As the summer advances this
seed-vessel grows larger and fatter and becomes
a fruit (6) called an acorn, which is a pale yellow
colour at first, and later is a dark olive brown.
The soft leafy cup hardens till it is firm as wood,
and in it the acorn sits fast till it is ripe. It
then falls from the cup and is greedily eaten by
the squirrels and dormice, as it was in the olden
times by the pigs. From those acorns that are

left lying on the ground all winter, under the withered leaves, will grow the tiny shoots of a new tree when the spring sunshine comes again.

The Oak tree is the most hospitable of trees: it is said that eleven hundred insects make their home in its kindly shelter. There are five kinds of houses, which are called galls, built by insects, and you can easily recognise these, and must look for them on the Oak tree. Sometimes on the hanging stamen catkins you will find little balls like currants with the catkin stem running through the centre. These are the homes of a tiny grub which is living inside the currant ball, and which will eat its way out as soon as it is ready to unfold its wings and fly.

Often at the end of an Oak twig you find a soft, spongy ball which is called an Oak apple. It is pinkish brown on the outside and is not very regular in shape. This ball is divided inside into several cells, and in each cell there lives a grub which will also become a fly before summer is over.

Sometimes if you look at the back of an Oak leaf you will see it covered with small red spangles which are fringed and hairy. These spangles each contain a small insect, and they cling to their spangled homes long after the leaves have fallen to the ground.

Another insect home or gall grows in the leaves, and this one is much larger, sometimes as big as a marble. It too is made by an insect which is living inside, and this is called a leaf gall.

There is still another insect which attacks the leaf buds and causes them to grow in a curious way. Instead of opening as usual, the bud proceeds to make layers of narrow-pointed green leaves which it lays tightly one above the other, like the leaves of an artichoke or the scales of a fir cone. If you cut one of these Oak cones in half you will find many small insects inside, which have caused the bud to grow in this strange way.

And there is one other oak gall you must note. When the leaves have all fallen and the twigs are brown and bare, you see clusters of hard brown balls growing on some of them. They are smooth and glossy and the colour of dried walnuts. These also have been made by an insect. Sometimes you see the tiny hole in the ball by which the grub has bored its way out. This kind of gall does great harm to the tree, as it uses up the sap that should nourish the young twigs.

The wood of the Oak is very valuable. Sometimes a fine old tree will be sold for four hundred pounds, and every part of it can be used. The bark is valuable because it contains large quantities of an acid which is used in making ink; also in dyeing leather. Oak that has been lying for years in a peat bog, where there is much iron in the water, is perfectly black when dug out, black as ink, because the acid and the iron together have made the inky colour.

The wood of an Oak tree lasts very long: there

are Oak beams in houses which are known to be
seven hundred years old, and which are as good
as the day they were cut. For centuries our
ships were built of Oak, the wooden walls of old
England, hearts of Oak, as they have often been
called, because Oak wood does not readily splinter
when struck by a cannon ball. And Oak wood
will not quickly rot: we know of piles which
have been driven into river beds centuries ago
and are still sound and strong. In pulling down
an old building lately in London, which was built
six hundred and fifty years ago, the workmen
found many oak piles in the foundations, and
these were still quite sound.

PLATE II

THE BEECH

In the south of England there lived a holy hermit
named St. Leonard whose hut was surrounded by
a glade of noble Beech trees. The saint loved the
beautiful trees, but by day he could not sit under
their shady branches because of the vipers which
swarmed about the roots, and by night the songs
of many nightingales disturbed his rest. So he
prayed that both the serpents and the birds might
be taken away, and from that day no viper has
stung and no nightingale has warbled in the
Hampshire forests. So we read in the old story

books. There are many such legends connected
with the Beech tree. It has grown in this country
as far back as we have any history, and it is often
called the mother of the forest, because its thickly
covered branches give shelter and protection to
younger trees which are struggling to live.

The Beech is a cousin of the Oak. It is a large,
handsome tree, with a noble trunk and widely
spreading branches which sweep downward to the
ground, and in summer every branch and twig is
densely covered with leaves. No other tree gives
such shade as the Beech, and in a hot summer day
how tempting it is to lie underneath the branches
and watch the squirrels glancing in and out among
the rustling leaves and tearing the young bark.

In early spring you will recognise the Beech
tree (1) by its smooth olive-grey trunk. Only the
Beech tree has such a smooth trunk when it is
fully grown, and in consequence, every boy with
a new knife tries to cut his name on its bark.
In summer the young bud (3) of next year's leaf
is formed where each leaf joins the stem. All
winter time you can see slender-pointed buds (4)
growing at the end of every twig, and when April
comes each of these pointed buds has become a
loose bunch of silky brown scales. Inside these
protecting scales is hidden the young leaf bud, and
soon the winter coverings unclose. For a short
time they hang like a fringe round the base of
the leaf stalk, but they quickly fall off and strew

the ground beneath. The young leaves inside are folded like a fan, and they have soft silky hairs along the edges. How lovely they are when open! Each leaf (2) is oval, with a blunted point at the end, and the edges are slightly waved.

At first the leaf colour is a clear pale green, through which the light seems to shine; and there is nothing more lovely than a Beech tree wood in early May when the young leaves are glistening against the clear blue sky. But as summer comes nearer the leaf colour darkens, and by July it is a deep, glossy green. You can then see very distinctly the veins which run from the centre to the edge of every leaf. These leaves grow so thickly that no stems or branches can be seen when the tree is in full foliage; and they are beautiful at all seasons. When autumn comes, bringing cold winds and a touch of frost, then the Beech tree leaves change colour: they seem to give us back again all the sunshine they have been storing up during summer, for they blaze like the sunset sky in myriad shades of gold, and red, and orange. In windy open places, these beautiful leaves soon strew the ground with a thick carpet that whirls and rustles in every breeze. But in sheltered glades, and especially in hedges, the leaves will hang all winter till they are pushed off by the new spring buds, and they glow russet red in the December sunshine, like the breast of the robin that is singing on the twig.

B

At every stage the Beech tree is a thing of beauty, and it is one of England's most precious possessions.

The young flowers appear about the same time as the leaves, and, like many other trees, the Beech has two kinds of flowers. The stamen flower (6) has a long, drooping stalk, from the end of which hangs a loose covering of fine brown scales, with pointed ends. Beyond this scaly covering hangs a tassel of purplish brown stamens, eight or twelve, or more, each with a yellow head.

On the same twig, not very far distant, you find the seed flower (5). This grows upright on a short stout stalk which bears at the end a bristly oval ball (7). At the top of this bristly ball you see six slender threads waving in the air. These rise from two seeds which are enclosed in the bristly covering. By and by the ball opens at the top and forms a cup with four prickly brown sides, each lined with silky green down. Inside the cup are two triangular green nuts which are the fruit (8). These nuts become dark brown when they ripen, and on windy days they are blown in thousands from their coverings and fall to the ground, where they lie hidden among the rustling brown leaves.

In old times people called these Beech nuts Beech-mast or food, and herds of pigs were taken to the Beech woods to feed on the nuts, which are said to contain oil. But pigs prefer to eat acorns, and nowadays the Beech nuts are left to fatten the squirrels and dormice, and the thrushes and deer, except those which children gather to string into necklaces.

No grass or plant will grow below the Beech tree branches: the leaves are too close together to let the sunshine reach the ground; also the roots are greedy, and are said to use up all the nourishment.

About a hundred years ago a Beech tree was found in Germany whose young leaves were dark purple red, and never became green. Young plants from this strange tree were much sought after, and now in many parts of the country you see red or copper beeches, as we usually call them.

Beech wood is used in various ways. In France the peasants make it into shoes—wooden shoes called sabots, which keep out the damp better than those made of any other wood. It is also used in shipbuilding and for making cheap furniture; but Beech wood is not nearly so valuable as that of the Oak, or Ash, or Elm.

PLATE III
THE BIRCH

" Sweet bird of the meadow, soft be thy nest,
    Thy mother will wake thee at morn from thy rest :
    She has made a soft nest, little redbreast, for thee,
    Of the leaves of the birch, and the moss of the tree."
                                                —Leyden.

The Birch tree is the daintiest and most fairy-like of all our forest trees, and, strange to say,

it is one of the hardiest. Who would believe that
the delicate tracery of purple twigs and branches,
which looks like fairy fretwork against the grey
wintry sky, could thrive in places where the sturdy
Oak tree dies ?

In the far, far north, in Lapland, where the
ground is snow-covered all the year, the Birch
tree flourishes, and many are the uses to which
it is put in that dreary land.

Look at the Birch tree (1) early in the year
before the sun has awakened the trees, and
flowers, and seeds from their long winter sleep.
It is easy to recognise, because no other tree
has such delicate twigs and branches, and the
colour of the trunk is peculiarly its own. Most
tree trunks are grey, or grey-green, or brown,
but the trunk of the Birch is covered with
a silvery white bark that glistens like satin.
In many places this bark is marked with dark
bands which crack across the tree trunk on the
silvery surface.

This silver bark is a wonderful thing. It peels
off readily in large flakes which resemble tissue
paper, and which look very easy to destroy, but
are wonderfully tough and lasting. It burns
readily, but in almost no other way can it be
destroyed. If a Birch tree is blown down and
left lying on the damp ground for many years,
all the wood inside the silvery bark will decay,
but the outside of the trunk remains unchanged.

PLATE II

THE BEECH

1. Beech Tree in Autumn   2. Leaf Spray   3. Bud
4. Buds in Winter   5. Seed Flower   6. Stamen Flower
7. Fruit   8. Fruit when Ripe

PLATE III

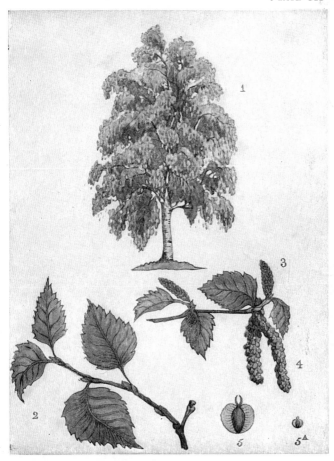

THE BIRCH

1. Birch Tree in Autumn   2. Leaf Spray   3. Seed Catkin
4. Stamen Catkin   5. Winged Seed enlarged
5A. Winged Seed natural Size

Stand on it, and you find that what you took to be a solid tree is nothing but a hollow tube of bark.

In North America the Indians cover their canoes with Birch bark, and in some snow-covered countries the people use it for tiles with which to roof their houses. Some time ago, when men were digging in the peat-bogs of Lancashire, they found the remains of Birch trees which must have been there for a thousand years. The wood had turned into stone, but the bark was still the same as when it grew on the tree.

In April the young leaves (2) cover the tree like a green mist. They are very tiny, the smallest and most fairy-like of all our tree leaves. Each leaf is oval in shape, with a glossy surface, and has a double row of teeth, first a large tooth, then a smaller one, cut unequally all round the edge. The leaf-stalk is very slender and wiry, and the twig to which it is attached is very little stouter, so that the leaves dance and rustle in the slightest breath of wind. Sometimes the back of a Birch leaf is covered with fine yellow powder. This powder is really a tiny plant which has made its home on the Birch tree leaf and feeds on it, just as the ivy and mistletoe do on larger trees. In autumn these leaves turn pale yellow, and the moss and heather are strewn with their flakes of gold.

There is another stranger makes its home on

some of the Birch trees. In spring, before the
leaves come, you may often notice curious bunches
of twigs that look like crows' nests high up
among the branches. These are caused by a
tiny insect which has come to stay on the Birch
tree, and, in some way which we do not understand, it makes all the twigs crowd together in
that curious manner. "Witches' Knots" they
are called in Scotland.

In May the Birch tree is in flower. You know
that tree flowers are not so easy to see as meadow
flowers : they require to be sought for and looked
at carefully if you wish to know about them.
The Birch tree has two kinds of flowers, and
both are needed if the seed from which new trees
may grow is to be made ready. It takes the
tree a whole year to prepare one kind of flower.
During summer look at the foot of a leaf stalk,
where it joins the twig, and you will find two tiny
green stamen catkins (4) with all their soft scales
tightly closed together. In autumn these little
catkins become dark purple, and they hang on
the tree all winter. Early in the following spring
they change entirely. The scales unclose and
the catkins grow longer till they look like a pair
of caterpillars loosely shaking in the wind.
Behind the scales in these reddy-brown caterpillars you find a mass of flowers, each made up
of one tiny sepal, also two slender stamens with
small yellow heads.

Now look at the other kind of flower, the seed catkin (3). These also are small and green, but they grow singly and are fatter and rounder than the stamen catkins. Their scales never open very wide, but if you look closely you will see behind each scale three little pear-shaped seed-vessels with two slender horns standing up from the top of each.

When the seeds in this catkin are ripe they resemble tiny nuts with wings on each side (5): and on windy days you can see clouds of these little winged seeds (5a) fluttering to the ground like small flies. Birds are very fond of Birch tree seeds, and one kind of finch, the siskin, is usually found hovering among the Birch trees.

The Birch tree lives till it is about a hundred years old. It is not grown up till it is twenty-five, so you will find no seeds on the young birches. It is a tree with many useful qualities. The bark is sometimes twisted into torches, as it contains a good deal of oil, and it is also used in tanning leather. The delicious scent of Russian leather is due to Birch bark oil. And there is sugar in the sap which may be made into wine. Furniture is largely made from the prettily grained Birch wood.

PLATE IV

THE ALDER

The Alder tree (1) is a cousin of the Birch and the Hazel, and like them its flowers and seeds are borne in catkins. It is usually to be found growing by the side of a slow-running stream, over which its slender branches bend gracefully, while its spreading roots cling to the boggy soil at the water's edge. For the Alder does not thrive in dry ground : it is a water-loving tree, and its many tiny roots attract moisture, and suck it up greedily; so that the ground where the Alder grows is often a marshy swamp.

Sometimes you will find an Alder which has grown into a lofty tree with a rough brown-black bark, and with many large branches; but it is much more frequently found as a low-growing and rather gloomy bush, about the same size as the Hazel.

The wood of the Alder is much sought after for buildings which stand in water. In Venice one of the most famous bridges, the Rialto, is built on piles, or great posts of Alder driven deep into the bed of the canal: and one reads in old history books that boats were first made of the trunks of the Alder tree. But it is of no use for fences or gate posts, as it decays quickly in dry soil.

If you watch a woodman cutting down an Alder

PLATE IV

THE ALDER

1. Alder Tree   2. Leaf Spray   3. Stamen Catkins
4. Seed Catkins   5. Last Year's Seed Catkins   6. Next Year's Stamen Catkins

tree you will notice that the chips which fall under his axe are very white; but soon they change colour and become a reddish pink. The hard wood knots which are found in the tree trunk are beautifully streaked and veined and are much prized by furniture makers.

In early spring you should walk to the banks of a stream and look for an Alder tree. Like the Hazel, you will easily know it by its winter catkins, though these are very different from Hazel catkins. Clinging to the boughs you see groups of small brown oval cones, which are quite hard and woody and which snap off easily. These woody cones are the withered seed catkins (5) of last year. As well as these you find bunches of long drooping caterpillars with tightly-shut purple-green scales, which will not unclose till the spring days come. These are the young stamen catkins, and they have taken six months to grow so far. By these you will always know the Alder tree; and it is most interesting to watch day by day how its catkins grow and change.

In spring the tree produces many groups of tiny seed catkins (4), which are hard and oval and covered with closely-shut green scales. As the days get warmer these cones grow larger and larger, and one day you will find the scales opening as a fir cone does when it is ripe. Underneath each scale are hidden two seeds, and from the top of each seed rise two slender horns. There are no wings to the seed, as in the Birch tree. These seed cones grow fatter and larger all summer, and by autumn their scales, instead of remaining green and soft, have become a dark reddish-brown colour and are hard and woody. In October or November the seed is quite ripe, and is shaken on to the boggy ground below. Then the empty seed catkins become dry and shrivelled, and they remain in groups clinging to the twigs all winter.

But the drooping caterpillars have been growing and changing too. Soon after the seed catkins have unclosed their hard oval balls, so that the sun and light may reach their tiny seeds, these drooping stamen catkins (3) unclose, and their scales take on a deeper shade of reddish purple. Each scale is edged with three points, and each point covers four tiny stamens and four tiny petals. When the fine powder in the yellow stamen heads is ripe, the wind blows it from the dangling tails on to the seed cones which are waiting for it, as without the stamen powder the seeds would never ripen: and soon after this happens the dangling tails fall to the ground.

If you look at an Alder tree in late autumn you will find three kinds of catkins. First, the empty seed catkins with dry woody scales; second, the dangling stamen catkins with the fine stamen dust all blown away: and third, there are tiny little caterpillar catkins with their scales still tightly closed together—these are next year's stamen catkins (6) just begun to form.

The leaves (2) of the Alder are heavy and leathery. They are usually rounded at the tips, but sometimes they are square, as if a piece had been cut off. Each leaf is prettily toothed all round the edge, and the veins, which run from the centre rib to the margin, are very much raised. When the leaves are newly opened, the underside is covered with tufts of soft down, and they are slightly sticky. Sometimes they are tinged with dull purple. These leaves are placed alternately on the stem, and while still in bud each leaf is enclosed in a pair of oval sheaths like small yellow ears. These ears do not fall off when the leaf unfolds, as do the leaf coverings of the Birch and the Beech; you will often find them at the bottom of the leaf stalk when the leaf is fully grown.

PLATE V

THE HORNBEAM

This is a tree that many people tell you they have never noticed; even people who know the names of most of our forest trees look surprised if you ask them which is the Hornbeam (1); they have never heard of it. And yet it grows freely in England in the woods and hedgerows, and like the Beech it is invaluable for sheltering with its close bushy branches younger trees that are struggling to live. If left to grow in good soil the Hornbeam will become a tall tree over seventy feet high, but it is not usual to find such well-grown Hornbeams, because the tree is generally planted to form hedges, and as these require thickness and bushiness rather than height, the top of the tree is often cut off, so that all its strength may go to producing side-branches.

Last century it was the fashion to have curious puzzle-paths made in gardens. You entered at a gap in a leafy hedge and walked on and on, and in and out between growing hedges till you came to an open space in the centre. Then the puzzle was to find your way out again, and this was sometimes very difficult. This kind of puzzle-path was called a maze, and the hedges of these mazes were frequently made of Hornbeam, because this tree will allow itself to be clipped and cut into any shape, and if its tall spreading branches are taken away, it at once puts out many small side-shoots which form a thick hedge.

The Hornbeam branches have a curious habit of growing together where they cross each other. You may find two good-sized branches which are separate on the lower part of the tree, but higher up they cross and touch each other, and frequently they join together and become one branch.

In the town of Ghent in Belgium there is a winding walk arched with Hornbeam : the trees have been planted so close that they meet overhead, and they have then been clipped and cut till they form a green tunnel under which you can walk for three hundred yards.

The trunk of the Hornbeam is a dull grey colour, and it is marked with white spots. It is not round, as are most tree trunks, but looks as if it had been slightly flattened, and so made oval when it was young. The leaves are not unlike those of the Elm and the young Beech, and when the tree is young it is sometimes mistaken for one or other of these. But you will notice some differences if you look carefully.

The Hornbeam leaf (2) is oval and tapers to a sharp point. It has strongly-marked veins running from the centre to the edge of the leaf, and these veins stand up like cord on the underside of the leaf. You remember that the Beech leaf was smooth and glossy, and that the Elm leaf was rough and hairy ? The Hornbeam comes just between the two : it is too rough to be a Beech leaf, and is also too pointed, and it is too smooth to be an Elm leaf. Besides, the two sides of the Hornbeam leaf meet exactly opposite each other on the leaf stalk, and in the Elm the one side of the leaf very often joins the stalk farther down than the other : the leaf is lopsided.

The Hornbeam leaves have two rows of teeth round the edge, and in autumn they turn yellow, and this yellow colour changes into red brown as the winter draws near. In sheltered places the leaves will hang on the branches all winter, till in spring they are pushed off by the young leaf buds.

The Hornbeam has two kinds of flowers, which grow in catkins, and both are found on the same tree. The stamen catkins (3) come with the young leaves early in April, and they grow on those twigs which were produced last year. It is not possible to mistake the Hornbeam for either the Beech or the Elm if you see the flowers, for neither of these has hanging catkins like the Hornbeam. Each catkin is made up of many green scales covering the catkin loosely. These scales are broad and oval, and they end in a sharp point. Hidden at the foot of each scale lies a thick bunch of yellow-headed stamens with no petals and no sepals around them. These yellow stamen heads end in tufts of fine hairs, and they are filled with pollen dust. As soon as this dust is ripe the yellow heads burst and scatter it over the seed flowers which have been mak‧ing ready to receive it. After this the stamen catkins shrivel, and they soon fall from the tree.

But there are other Hornbeam flowers, also growing in catkins (4) which appear at the end of this year's young twigs. Each catkin is covered with soft, silky spear leaves, and behind every three of these narrow leaves there nestles a tiny seed with two little horns standing up at the top. These silky leaves soon fall off and are replaced by others which are very different. These are called bracts, and they look like a small hand with one long finger and two much shorter fingers. They are covered with a network of fine veins, and inside the hand sits the fruit (5), a small three-sided nut. When you see a bushy, drooping cluster of these green leafy bracts, each with its nut at the foot, you wonder how any one could mistake the Hornbeam for either the Beech or the Elm.

You will often see a dainty little bird called the hawfinch sitting on the Hornbeam branches and eating the nuts.

The wood of this tree is said to be very hard. Joiners do not care to work on Hornbeam, as it quickly blunts their tools; and some people tell you that the name is really Hard-beam, and that we have got into a careless habit of calling the tree by a wrong name. But there is another tale which may be the true one. Long ago, when ploughing was done by bullocks in this country, as it is to-day in many lands, each pair of bullocks was fastened together with a wooden collar called a yoke. This yoke was made of Hornbeam because of its strength, and the tree might get its name because from it was made the beam of wood that goes over the horns.

Nowadays the wood is little used except for making small things, such as handles of knives, and spoons, and cog-wheels.

PLATE VI

THE HAZEL

There are few of us who think of the Hazel as one of our forest trees. We know it as a large, straggling bush, with a thicket of leaves and branches, among which are hidden delicious nuts. But in some places the Hazel has quite outgrown the bush stage: in Middlesex there is a Hazel tree sixty feet high, with a straight thick trunk and many large branches covered luxuriantly with leaves.

The Hazel (1) has been known in history for many centuries. The Romans wrote that its spreading roots did harm to the young vines, but they found its supple twigs invaluable for tying up the straggling vine shoots.

Scotland is said to have been called Caledonia from Cal Dun, which means the hill of Hazel. And in Surrey we have the name Haslemere, which tells its own story.

In damp places beside streams, or on light soil close to quarries, or among broken rocky

PLATE V

THE HORNBEAM

1. Hornbeam   2. Leaf Spray   3. Stamen Catkin
4. Seed Catkin   5. Fruit

ground, the Hazel thrives, and many are the happy afternoons spent by children of all ages gathering nuts in the Hazel coppice. This is the only tree we have which produces food good to eat in its wild state.

You will not find the Hazel difficult to recognise at any time of year. Before the month of January is over you will notice a pair of long brown caterpillars dangling in the wind from many of the Hazel twigs: lamb's tails, the country children call them, but their correct name is Hazel catkins; and like those of the Birch tree, they have been hanging on the tree all winter, but were so small that you did not notice them.

In summer, if you look carefully, you find many tiny green stamen catkins growing between the foot of the leaf stalk and the branch. These green cones grow very, very slowly all autumn and winter, and when January is nearly over they change into these dangling tails or hanging catkins (3), and their tightly-folded scales begin to unclose. Behind these scales lie eight stamens, each of which has a bright yellow head. These yellow heads are filled with fine powder, and when ripe they burst, and the fine powder is shaken out by the wind. Soon after, the catkin turns brown and shrivelled, and before very long it falls off; its work for the year is over.

When the snowdrops bloom, in the end of January, the other Hazel flowers or seed catkins

D

are ready. They are not easily seen, so you must look for them carefully. On each side of the stalk you will find a small scale-covered bud (4), and at the tip of this bud rises a tuft of crimson threads. Inside this scale-covered bud are the seeds, and from the top of each seed rise two crimson threads. On windy days the fine powder from the yellow stamen heads is shaken over these crimson threads, which carry it to the young seeds hidden beneath the scaly covering. As spring advances this crimson tuft disappears and the bud busies itself making the seed, which must be ready by autumn. The covering of the seed hardens like a nut: at first this nut is pale green, but in winter it becomes a glossy russet brown.

Inside this nut (5) lies the kernel of the seed, and it is this sweet kernel which is the fruit we eat. Meantime the scaly leaves, which formed the covering of the young bud, have grown much larger: they have become tough and leathery, and their ends are deeply divided, as if they were torn. In the Filbert Hazel, which is a cousin of the common Hazel and very like it, these leathery coverings conceal the nut. But in the common or Cobnut Hazel they form a cup in which the nut sits in the same way as the acorn does in its cup.

The leaves (2) of the Hazel appear in early spring. They are rounded leaves, sometimes slightly heart-shaped, and they have two rows of teeth cut round the edge. Each leaf is rough and hairy, and is covered with a network of veins which seems to pucker the leaf. At first the young leaf stalk and branches are covered with fine down, but this soon wears off. Notice how many long, straight shoots rise from the ground beside the Hazel roots. On these Hazel shoots the leaves are placed in two rows on each side of the shoot, with the leaves not opposite each other, but alternate. The shoots make good baskets, and hoops, and hurdles, because they can be so easily bent into many shapes without breaking. The branches of the Hazel bush have the same good qualities, and they are valuable for fishing rods and walking sticks, and such purposes, where toughness and elasticity are needed.

The Hazel leaves hang longer on the tree than most other leaves. The frost changes their colour from a dull grey-green to a pale yellow, but still they cling to their stalks till the winter wind strips them from the branches.

It is said that Hazel shoots or twigs have the power of showing where water is concealed. In places where there are no lakes, or rivers, or streams near at hand, water is got by digging wells deep down into the ground, and so allowing the stores which are hidden there to rise to the surface. But it is not everywhere that these hidden supplies will be found, and as digging a well costs a great deal of money, people are unwilling to begin the work unless they are likely to succeed. So they send for a man who is called a diviner, because he divines or guesses where water will be found. He walks across the fields carrying a Hazel rod in his hand, and when he reaches a spot where water lies beneath, the Hazel rod changes position in his hand and the well is sunk at the spot which the diviner points out. So the story goes.

For many generations it was a custom in this country to burn Hazel nuts on the night of October 31, All-Hallow Eve. Friends would meet together late in the evening, and each person would place two nuts as near together as possible in a clear red fire. The nuts were supposed to represent the two friends, and if they burned quietly and evenly, then the future was sure to be happy; but if they flared angrily or sputtered hissingly, especially if they burst with a loud report, then misfortune was supposed to follow the friends.

Hazel nuts are eagerly devoured by squirrels and dormice, and there is one bird, the Nuthatch, that is very busy and grows sleek and fat when the Hazel fruit is ripe. This bird breaks off a nut branch and flies away with it to an old oak tree. There he strips off the covering of leaves and cleverly places the bare nut in a crevice of the rough oak trunk. Then with his strong bill he hammers at the shell till it breaks and he can get at the nut inside. On still October days

PLATE VI

THE HAZEL

1. Hazel Bush   2. Leaf Spray with Nuts   3. Stamen Catkin
        4. Seed Catkins   5. Hazel Nuts

PLATE VII

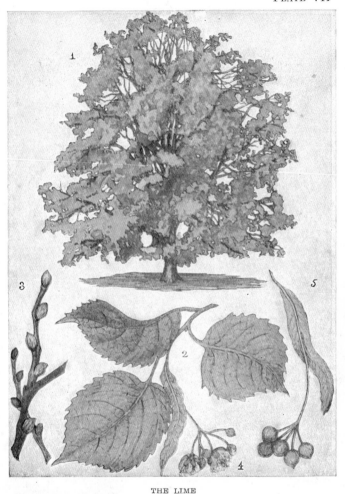

THE LIME

1. Lime Tree   2. Leaf Spray with Flowers   3. Pink Buds

4. Flower Cluster   5. Fruit with Bract

in the quiet woods you will hear his bill tap-tapping from the trunk of the oak tree.

PLATE VII

THE LIME OR LINDEN

"The Lime, a summer home of murmurous wings."
—Tennyson.

The Lime or Linden (1) is one of the most
familiar trees in our large towns. It is very
hardy, and you find it planted by the side of our
smoky streets, where it seems to thrive in spite
of the clouds of sooty dust that cover its delicate
leaves.

But if you wish to know what a Lime tree
really looks like at its best, then you must find
one growing in some country park where there
is space, and fresh air, and plenty of sunshine;
then you will see how beautiful a tree it can be.
The Lime is a tall, stately tree. It has many
slender branches closely covered with leaves, which
have each a long stalk. In old trees the branches
often bend down close to the ground, but the
sunshine always succeeds in finding its way under
the Lime tree branches, and it flickers on the
grass as it never does beneath the Beech tree
boughs.

In winter the Lime tree is difficult to recognise,

although there is one feature you may notice: its bare stems and twigs are very black against the sky, and many of the branches hang so awkwardly that they look as if they were dead. But go to the park in spring, and at once you will know which is the Lime tree. Every little twig is coloured a delicate shade of olive green tinged with crimson, and bears many small oval buds (3) which are red like rubies. In May these ruby buds burst open, and their crimson coverings fall to the ground, disclosing the pale emerald-green leaf that is tightly folded within. The leaves (2) soon open in the sunshine, and you see that each is shaped like a large pointed heart, and that the two sides of the heart are uneven.

The edge of the leaf is cut into sharp teeth, and all over it a network of fine veins is spread. When the leaf is still young you find tufts of soft, downy hairs on the underside, and at first each leaf hangs straight down from its stalk as if it had not strength to rise and face the sunlight. But they soon raise themselves, and gradually their pale green colour darkens, though the Lime tree leaf never becomes so dark, nor is it as glossy, as the leaf of the Beech tree.

In September the Lime tree leaves turn pale yellow: rather a colourless yellow, very different from the rich gold and red-brown of the Beech, and they fall with the first touch of frost.

You may sometimes find leaves which are

marked with large black, sooty-looking spots. These spots are caused by a tiny insect which has made its home on the leaf.

If you sit beneath the branches of the Lime on a warm summer day you will hear the constant hum of myriads of bees which are buzzing round the tree. They are gathering honey from the Lime tree flowers, whose delicious perfume is scenting the air.

From the spot where next year's leaf bud will grow there hangs a long stalk; at the end of this stalk there droops a cluster of flowers (4), and at the base of each flower cluster stands a long slender leaf called a bract. This bract looks like a pale yellow wing, and is covered all over with a network of fine veins.

The flowers have five greeny white petals and five pale green sepals. In the centre is a small seed-vessel like a tiny pea, and from it there rises a slender green pillar which ends in five sticky points. Closely surrounding this seed-vessel is a ring of many stamens. Each stamen has a white stalk with an orange-coloured head, and among these stamens lie the drops of sweet juice which attract the bees.

The stamen dust is ripe before the sticky points of the seed-vessel on the same plant are ready for it; but the bees, when they bend down to suck the honey juice, brush against the ripe stamen heads, and their backs become covered with the fine powder. Away they fly to the flowers on another Lime tree, and the powder will probably be rubbed off on one where the seed-vessel is ready to receive it.

When the seed is ripe you see many little downy fruit-balls (5), each hanging from a slender stalk. In warm countries this seed ripens into a small nut which is ground down and made into a kind of chocolate. But it never ripens in England.

In some countries there are large forests of Lime trees, and the air is filled with the busy hum of the bees. The peasants make large holes in the tree trunks, and these holes the bees fill with honeycomb, which the peasants easily remove and sell. This Lime tree honey is much prized for its fine flavour.

The wood of the Lime tree is not hard enough for building purposes, but it is greatly in demand for carving. It is light and soft, and much of the beautiful wood decoration in our churches is carved from Lime tree wood. It does not easily become worm-eaten as do so many of our harder woods.

We read that in old days the soldiers' shields were made of Lime tree wood, as the blow of a weapon was deadened when striking it.

The inner bark of the tree has always been valuable. From it are made those mats of light brown grass which gardeners use to protect their delicate plants during winter; and these tails

PLATE VIII

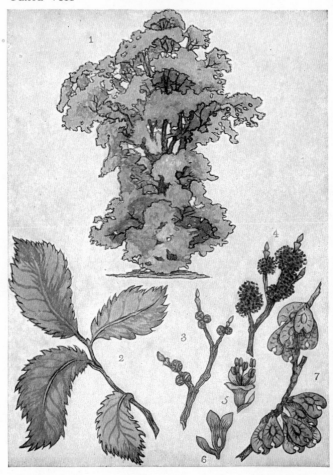

THE ELM

1. Elm Tree   2. Leaf Spray   3. Beady Buds
4. Flower Spray   5. Stamen Flower enlarged
6. Seed Flower enlarged   7. Fruit Clusters and Wing

of dried-looking grass with which they tie bunches of flowers instead of using string, are also made from the Lime tree bark. This inner bark is called "bass" or "bast," and is chiefly made in Russia and Sweden.

It is from this bass or string that the tree gets its name, which is not really Lime, but Line or Linden, and is so called in other countries. We in Britain have got into the bad habit of mis-pronouncing the word. The true Lime tree is a cousin of the Orange and Lemon trees, and bears a yellow fruit called Limes. But the Linden tree is no relation of this Lime tree, and is so called because it is the tree from which we get gardener's dried string or line, and we must remember that our popular name is a wrong one, and not the true name of the tree.

PLATE VIII

THE COMMON ELM AND WYCH OR BROAD-LEAVED ELM

There are two kinds of Elm which grow abundantly in this country, and both are lofty, noble trees. The Common Elm (1) you will recognise easily, because its rough black trunk is clothed right down to the ground with a dense mass of brushwood. This brushwood is really a forest of small branches, and shoots, and twigs which spring from the Elm tree root; and if you separate some of these young shoots and plant them alone they will grow into young Elm tree saplings.

In winter you will always know the Common Elm by its brushwood clothing, and in early spring, in March, after there have been a few sunny days, you will see tiny green leaf buds opening in this brushwood sheaf before the large upper branches show any signs of life.

The Common Elm is one of our tallest trees. It has a thick rough trunk, on which are many large gnarled bosses or knobs. The bark of the tree is very rugged and is covered with many deep furrows.

The branches of this Elm do not grow gracefully in sweeping curves like those of the Ash tree; they have a dwarf, zig-zag appearance, and often they are twisted and knotted.

The young twigs that grow on these branches are short and tiny, a network of little bushy sprays growing close to the branch, and their bark is downy and corky when it is young, but becomes hard as the season advances.

In early spring these tiny twigs bear many small scaly buds (3) like beads. These beads open very early, before the end of April, and from each there bursts a bunch of flowers (4). What you notice first in this flower tuft is the crowd of reddish stamens with large purple heads. But if you gently pull to pieces one of these flower bunches, you will find that the stamens are not growing loose, but that they are held together in groups of five or more, in a dark green or purplish vase (5). This vase is funnel-shaped, and widens out round the mouth into four scallops. The oval seed-vessel (6) is at the bottom, hidden from sight. Do not forget to notice that in the Elm tree the stamens and seed-vessel grow close together in one flower.

The stamens soon shrivel and fall off, and their place is taken by bunches of flat green wings (7), each with a tiny knob in the centre, which is the fruit. These green shields, or wings, serve the same purpose as the keys or wings of the Ash tree. They are thin and light like paper, and in the Common Elm each shield is deeply notched at one end, almost to the centre seed.

When the seed is ripe the wind blows these bunches of papery shields away from the twigs, and they are carried long distances.

The Elm tree seed is almost ripe before the leaves (2) begin to sprout. The leaf buds are pink and downy, and the young leaves are folded fanways inside. Each leaf has a short stalk, and is small and narrow, with two rows of unequally-sized teeth round the edge. These leaves are rough and harsh above, with many hairs along the centre rib, hairs like those on the Nettle, which is a member of the same family as the Elm, but these hairs, though they irritate, do not actually sting. In October the leaves turn yellow, and after a touch of frost they fall in showers.

Sometimes you will notice large black spots disfiguring the leaves. These spots are caused by a minute plant which makes its home on the leaf and in the end destroys it. After the leaves have fallen, they lie on the ground till spring comes again, then this black plant increases rapidly, and soon covers all the leaf, which quickly decays.

Cattle love the Elm tree leaves when they are green and young, and in some places they are stripped from the trees in sackfuls to feed the cows.

Many insects make their home on the Elm tree. The caterpillar of the large tortoise-shell butterfly feeds on the leaves, and there is an insect beetle that burrows little tunnels in the wood and loosens the bark from the tree. If you pick up some pieces of Elm tree wood where a woodman has been sawing, you will see curious markings like the veins of a skeleton leaf, tunnelled in the wood. These are made by a tiny beetle, and are very injurious to the tree.

But the beetle has an enemy that comes to the tree's rescue. Sometimes on a still day if you are sitting quietly in the woods, you will hear a gentle tap-tapping close beside you. This is the woodpecker, a bird which is perched on the rough bark of the Elm tree, and with his bill he pecks at the tree in search of insects which form his favourite meal.

Birds love the Elm trees, as their shade is not too dense to shut out the sunshine, and you will often find rooks' nests in the upper branches, tossed and swayed by the gales.

The Elm tree is useful for many purposes. Farmers plant it in their hedgerows, as grass will grow freely above its roots.

In Italy the Elms are trained to carry the Vines. The young trees have all their lower branches cut off, leaving the bare stem like a living pole; round this pole the slender vine is twined, and its graceful trails hang in festoons from the crown of Elm branches which are left at the top of the pole to give shade. In poetry you read of the Vine tree wedded to the common Elm, which it clasps with its clinging arms.

Elm tree wood is very valuable as timber. These rough bosses which grow on the trunk are prized by cabinet-makers, who find the wood curiously veined and streaked.

The inner lining of the bark is very tough, and is made into ropes and garden string or bast, as in the Lime tree. And the wood is sought for all purposes where durability is needed; it lasts well in water, and is much in demand for ship-building.

The Wych Elm or Broad-leaved Elm resembles the Common Elm in many ways, but there are several small differences you must note. There is no brushwood sheaf clothing the base of the Wych Elm trunk; it is bare and rough right down to the ground. The leaves are larger and much broader, resembling those of the Hazel, and the branches of the Wych Elm are long and spreading and much more graceful than the twisted boughs of its sister Elm.

If you look carefully at the green wings that surround the tiny seed of the Wych Elm and compare it with those of the Common Elm, you will find that the seed lies nearly in the centre of the wing, and that the notch which is cut at the end of the wing is smaller than the deep notch of the Common Elm.

The Wych Elm is far the more graceful of the two trees, and it grows much more quickly than its rugged sister.

The name Wych is supposed to be Scotch. Small pieces of the wood were said to be effective as charms against witches, and country dairymaids used to place a tiny bit of this Elm wood in the churn so that the witches could not prevent the milk from becoming butter!

PLATE IX

THE ASH

> " If the oak before the ash,
>   Then you'll only have a splash ;
>   If the ash before the oak,
>   Then you're sure to have a soak."
>   —Old Saying.

If the Oak is well named the King of the woods, to the Ash belongs the honour of being called Queen, the wood's fairest. She is a queen with an ancient history. In the dim long ago there must have been Ash trees, for we read that the great spear of Achilles was an "ashen spear"; also, that the gods held council under the boughs of a great Ash tree: on its highest branches sat an eagle; round its root a serpent lay coiled; and a tiny squirrel ran up and down the branches carrying messages from one to the other.

In much later times the Ash tree was held to have magic powers of healing. Sick babies were said to be cured if they passed through a cleft made in its trunk; and there are many tales of men and animals who recovered from illness on touching an Ash twig gathered from a tree in which a shrew mouse had been buried.

Nowadays we have grown so wise that we think differently about these things, and we love the Ash tree because of its beauty, and are grateful for the many ways in which the wood is useful to us.

You should try to find an Ash tree (1) in early spring. It is one of the easiest trees to recognise before it is clothed in leaves.

The trunk is very straight, and has none of the knobs and bosses which grow on the Oak and Elm tree trunks. When the Ash tree is still young the bark is a pale grey colour—ash-colour, we call it—and it is very smooth. But as the tree grows older the bark cracks into many irregular upright ridges, which remind you of the rimples left by the waves on a sandy sea-shore.

At first the lower branches grow straight out from the trunk, but soon they curve gracefully downwards; then they rise again, and the tips point upward toward the sky.

Notice the tips of these branches—they are quite different from all other tree tips. In an Ash tree you will not see a network of delicate branching twigs outlined against the sky. Each branch ends in a stout pale grey twig, which is slightly flattened at the tip, as if it had been pinched between two fingers when still soft. Beyond this flattened tip you see two fat black buds (4), and there are smaller black buds at the sides of the twig. It is these curious black buds at the tips and on the sides of the twig which will make it easy for you to distinguish the Ash tree from every other.

Long after the other trees have put on their

PLATE IX

THE ASH

1. Ash Tree
4. Black Buds
7. Seed enlarged

2. Leaf Spray
5. Leaf Scars

3. "Keys" or "Spinners." Ash Fruit
6. Stamen enlarged

8. Ash Flowers

young green leaves the Ash tree stands bare and leafless, waiting till the frost and cold winds are gone before its black buds will unfold. Then out it comes, flowers first. The sooty buds at the sides of the twig open, and you see that they have dark brown linings, and that in the middle of each bud there lies a thick bunch of purple stamen heads (6), crowded together like grains of purple corn; these are the Ash tree flowers (8).

Ash tree flowers have no petals and no sepals; they have only a green, bottle-shaped seed-vessel (7), which stands between two stamens with pale green stalks and fat purple-coloured heads. Sometimes there is not even a seed-vessel; you may find nothing but a crowded bunch of purply stamens. This latter kind of Ash tree cannot produce any fruit.

In a few weeks these stamens shrivel and the purple heads fall off. The seed-vessels, too, become very different. They change into long flat green wings, which hang each from its own stalk in a cluster at the end or from the side of the branch. These silky green wings are called "keys" (3), or in some places, "spinners"; at one end they are notched, and at the other, close to the stalk, lies the fruit. Long after the Ash tree leaves are withered and fallen you can see these bunches of "keys," grown brown and shrivelled, still clinging to the branches. When wintry weather comes they are torn off by the wind, and the winged seed, spinning round and round in the air, is carried a long distance.

You will see Ash trees growing high up on rocky precipices, where only the birds or the wind could have left the seed.

By the month of May, when the keys of the Ash are fully formed, the green leaves (2) begin to appear. They are beautiful feathery leaves, full of lightness, and grace, and strength. Each leaf is made up of from four to eleven pairs of leaflets, shaped like a lance, with toothed edges, and these are placed opposite each other on a central stalk: there is nearly always a single leaflet at the end. The leaves are pale green, and when they first open you see a soft browny down on the leaf ribs, but this soon wears off. They droop gracefully from the twigs, which you can now see require to be stout and strong to carry such large wind-tossed feathers.

But the Ash tree leaves are among the first to fall. Whenever the cold winds come they wither, and a single night of frost will strew them in hundreds on the ground. Where the leaf stalk joined the twig you will see a curious scar (5) shaped like a horse-shoe, and next year a black bud will appear inside this scar. The Ash tree will live for several hundred years. It is not fully grown up till it is forty or fifty years old, and till then you will not find any bunches of keys, with their seeds, growing on the tree.

Notice that the ground beneath the branches of the Ash tree is usually bare. Many of its roots spread out to a great distance close below the surface, and they are so greedy, and require so much nourishment for the tree, that there is none left for other plants. Some farmers think that the raindrops which drip from the feathery Ash leaves are hurtful to other plants, so they are unwilling to plant Ash trees in their fields and hedgerows.

The wood of the Ash is very valuable, and will bring as much money as that of the Oak or Elm. It is used for all kinds of work—for furniture and for ship-building, and for making wheels and poles, and it lasts well and does not readily split.

PLATE X

THE FIELD MAPLE

There are many mistakes made in naming the Maple and Plane trees. The Sycamore or False Plane tree, the Oriental Plane, and the Field Maple are often called wrongly by each other's names. So you must note carefully the differences between them. The Sycamore and the Field Maple are cousins, but the Oriental Plane is not even a distant relation of these, and only resembles them in the shape of its leaves. It is not really difficult to distinguish one from the other.

The Field Maple (1) is nearly always a small tree which you find growing in the hedgerows, where it is more like a large bush than a tree. You rarely find it standing alone in a wide park, bearing great branches heavily clothed with leaves, as you find the Sycamore or Great Maple. In England it is a common hedgerow tree, but it is not native to Scotland and is seldom found there.

Early in spring you find the long slender shoots covered with buds, from which burst small leaves of a beautiful bright crimson colour. These leaves (2) are toothed round the edges and are shaped like a hand with five short fingers; in the Field Maple the fingers are blunt at the points, not sharp as are those of the Sycamore and of the Oriental Plane.

As the spring advances those pretty crimson leaves become dark green above and a light green on the under-side, and they lose the soft down which covered them, but even when fully out they are never so large as those of the Sycamore. When autumn draws near, with its cold winds and frosty nights, the Field Maple leaves change colour once more and become brilliant yellow; you will see them shining in the hedgerows like a bush of gold.

Many of the leaves are disfigured by small red spots, and if you look at one of these spots with

PLATE X

THE FIELD MAPLE

1. Field Maple in Autumn   2. Leaf Spray   3. Flower Spike   4. Fruit

PLATE XI

THE SYCAMORE

1. Sycamore Tree   2. Leaf Spray   3. Fat Bud
4. Flower Spike   5. Winged Fruit

a magnifying glass you will see that it is caused by a tiny insect which has made this little red nest in which to lay its eggs.

The leaves of the Field Maple, like those of the Sycamore, are placed opposite each other on the twig; in the Oriental Plane they grow alternately, one a little way above the other on opposite sides of the spray. There is a great deal of sugary juice in Maple leaves, and cattle love to eat them. In some countries they are stripped from the trees and kept for winter fodder for the cows.

The bark of the Field Maple is noted for its strange corky nature and its curious growth. It grows in upright ridges, deeply furrowed, which look as if they could easily be broken off. In the Oriental Plane the bark is quite smooth, and it peels off in large flakes, leaving patches of different colours on the tree trunk.

In April, when the leaves are still unfolding, the Field Maple brings out its spikes of flowers (3). You will at once notice that these flower clusters stand erect, and do not droop in pointed tassels like those of the Sycamore. Now, look at the flowers in an Oriental Plane, and you will discover that they bear no resemblance either to those of the Sycamore or of the Field Maple, with which it is often confused. They do not even grow in clusters, but in round, prickly balls which are threaded on a slender green chain.

The flowers of the Field Maple are what botanists call " perfect flowers," which means that each flower has all its parts complete within itself. In every bloom you will find five narrow green sepals and five narrow green petals; within the ring of petals stand eight yellow-headed stamens, and seated in the centre of the flower is a seed-vessel with a small wing at each side and with two curly horns standing up at the top. There is plenty of honey juice hidden among these stamens, and the bees buzz all day long around the Maple blossoms.

As the season advances, the petals and sepals and stamens fall off, but the seed-vessel grows larger and larger, till you find bunches of winged seeds (4) standing erect where the flowers once grew.

Notice that in this tree the seeds are close together beside the stalk, and that the wings stand straight out from the seeds and are not bent into the shape of the letter U, as they are in the Sycamore. These bunches of winged seeds are frequently tinged with bright crimson, and are very attractive among the glossy green leaves.

In autumn the strong winds strip them from their stalks and the wings bear the seed far from the parent tree. Some botanists tell us that these seeds require to lie in the ground for more than a year before they begin to grow.

The Field Maple is full of sugary sap, but

nothing is made of it in this country, as the trees do not yield enough to make it worth while. But in Canada the sap is drawn from the trees and made into sugar. I am sure you must have seen the brown blocks of Maple sugar in the confectioners' windows.

The wood of the Field Maple is too small to be of much use, but it is strangely and beautifully marked and veined with spots and stripes like the skin of a tiger or panther, and is eagerly bought for decorative purposes. The knots that grow on the roots were said to be worth their weight in gold, and in old history books you read that the thrones of great kings were made of Maple. Nowadays the wood is largely used for making small articles such as plates, and cups, and trays, and it can be cut so thin without breaking that the light may be seen through it.

In France the long slender Maple shoots are used for coachmen's whips.

PLATE XI

THE SYCAMORE, OR GREAT MAPLE, OR MOCK PLANE

There is a good deal of confusion in people's minds as to the right name for this familiar tree. Sycamore is not an English word, but is made

from a Greek word meaning fig or mulberry. The
tree has been so called because many years ago
people believed that it was a relation of the fig
tree which grows so abundantly by the roadside in
Palestine. The leaves are a little alike, but there
is no real resemblance between our English
Great Maple and the Eastern Sycamore: the
name has been given by mistake.

Another mistaken name given to this tree is
Plane tree. The Great Maple is only a mock
Plane tree or false Plane tree; it is not even a
relation of the real Plane any more than it is a
relation of the Fig or Sycamore. But mistakes
even in names are very difficult to correct, and
in many places, particularly in Scotland, you will
find that Sycamore (1) or Plane tree is the name
usually given to the Great Maple.

It is a large heavy tree, with a great central
trunk covered with a gnarled bark which peels
off in flakes, leaving patches of different shades.
From every side of this central trunk there grow
stout branches covered with masses of thick
foliage, the thickest and heaviest foliage of any
British tree.

If you look at the Sycamore tree as it stands
in an open field, or in a hedgerow, with grass
growing close to its very trunk, I think what
will strike you most is how evenly it has grown
all round. There are so many trees that grow
all to one side if they are much exposed to a

cold wind. Look at the Beech, or the Hawthorn, or the Elm on the crest of a ridge, and you will at once know from which direction the wind blows strongest and coldest, by seeing how the tree puts out all its best branches on the sheltered side. But the Sycamore tree is indifferent to cold, or even to the salt sea winds; it sends out its branches equally on every side, and there is always a thick roof of leaves at the top.

The Sycamore tree prefers a dry soil, in which it grows very quickly; and it will not die if transplanted.

In early spring the twigs bear many large fat buds (3), which are covered with soft downy pink scales. The Horse Chestnut is the only other tree which bears such large buds, but they are dark and very sticky.

In country places the children call the largest buds at the end of the Sycamore twig "cocks," and the smaller buds which grow along the sides they call "hens." When these buds open early in May you see how beautifully the leaves are folded fan-ways inside. Each leaf (2) is shaped like a large hand with five bluntly-pointed fingers; the edges are coarsely toothed, and the leaf is dark green above and a paler green underneath. They grow on long stalks, which are a reddish pink colour so long as the leaves are young, and each stalk is scooped into a hollow at the end, so that it may fit closely to the twig.

G

These leaves are not placed alternately on opposite sides of the branch, as in the Beech or Elm: they grow in clumps, or bouquets, and each pair of leaves is placed crossways to the pair above. Those that come out first have long stalks and are the largest; then the second pair is smaller, and the third pair smaller still, till the bouquet is finished with two tiny leaves in the centre.

Notice that the leaves of the Sycamore are often marked with sticky drops. By old writers these drops are called honey-dew. It is believed that the sap of the Sycamore is sugary, and some of this sugary juice escapes through the leaf pores to the surface. These handsome leaves are often spotted with small black dots, which are caused by a tiny plant. This plant makes its home on the Sycamore leaf, and unknowingly disfigures its kind host.

Before the leaves are quite out the flowers appear. They grow in drooping spikes (4), or large tassels of a pale yellowish green colour. Each tassel is made up of many separate flowers, and most of these flowers have a calyx with five to twelve narrow strap-shaped sepals, and a corolla of the same number of yellow-green petals. There is also a ring of slender stamens standing round a flat green cushion or disc. In the centre sits the seed-vessel, which has two curved horns at the top. But in the flower tassel you may also find flowers in which some of the parts are awanting: one flower will have stamens, but no seed-vessel, and its neighbour will have a seed-vessel and no stamens, while in a third the petals may be awanting. You must examine each flower till you find one which is perfect. These Sycamore flowers contain much honey, nearly as much as those of the Lime tree; and the bees are glad to hover round the tree flowers, which blossom long before those in the meadow are open.

After the flowers are withered the seed (5) develops wings like the Ash and the Elm. But these wings are very different from those of any other tree. They are shaped like the letter U, with the two seeds at the bottom of the letter where it joins the stalk. Each seed is like a small pea, and is snugly packed in a horny case lined with the softest and silkiest down. When it is ripe the wind blows the winged seeds from the tree and carries them a long way. They fall into the ground, where the horny case prevents the young seed from rotting during the cold winter months before it is time for it to begin to sprout. Then when spring comes the baby seed bursts its covering and sends up two tiny green ribbon leaves which are the beginning of a new Sycamore tree. The wings of the Sycamore seed are beautifully tinged with pink.

The wood of the Sycamore or Great Maple is white and very soft, but it is closely grained.

Sometimes you see big knobs on the tree trunk where a branch has died or been broken off, and cabinet-makers prize these knobs, as the wood is very curiously marked with beautiful veins and streaks. Maple wood will polish as smooth as satin, and the backs of violins are often made of it. In old books we read of table-tops that were made of curiously marked pieces of Maple, and it is told that more than eight hundred pounds was given for one of these Maple tables.

In Scotland the Sycamore tree was often called the dool tree, or tree of mourning, because the nobles used to hang disobedient servants or vanquished foes on its strong branches; and at Cassilis, in Ayrshire, there is a Sycamore tree which is well known to have been used for this cruel purpose.

PLATE XII

THE ORIENTAL PLANE

There are two kinds of Plane tree which have come to us as strangers from foreign lands and have taken kindly to our cold climate and biting winds. These are the Oriental or Eastern Plane and the Occidental or Western Plane. The differences between them are not great, and the one which you will most easily remember is, that in the Oriental Plane the leaf stalk is green, whereas

PLATE XII

THE ORIENTAL PLANE TREE

1. Oriental Plane Tree   2. Leaf Spray   8. Stamen Flower Balls
4. Seed Flower Balls   5. Fruit

PLATE XIII

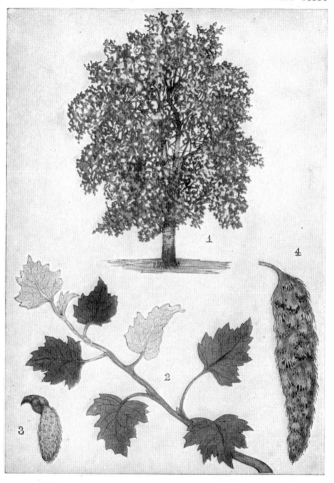

THE WHITE POPLAR

1. White Poplar or Abele Tree   2. Leaf Spray
3. Seed Catkin   4 Stamen Catkin

in the Occidental Plane tree it is purply red. We owe a special debt of gratitude to these Plane trees because they add beauty to so many of the dingy streets and squares in our big cities.

The trunk of the Oriental Plane (1) is very smooth, and is usually ash-grey in colour; sometimes it is a very dark green. The outer layer of this trunk peels off in flakes, leaving large patches of greenish yellow, and these give the tree a curious speckled appearance. It is a tall, handsome tree, and if you look at it from a distance you see that the broad leaves group themselves into large masses with a wide space between each mass. This you can only see in a full-grown tree, and such trees are rarely met with in our dusty towns.

On account of its leaves the Oriental Plane tree is frequently confused with the Sycamore, so you must notice carefully wherein they differ. The leaves (2) of the Oriental Plane are shaped like a hand with five sharply-pointed fingers, and each finger is cut all round into sharp teeth. The leaves are very smooth, and light, and fine, and are as thin as paper. They will lie quite flat if you lay them on a table. Each leaf is placed alternately with its neighbour on the twig, the second leaf growing on the opposite side of the twig, but a little further up than the first leaf. In the Sycamore you remember that the leaves grow in pairs placed exactly opposite each other, and that the second pair is always placed cross-ways to the first pair? These Oriental Plane leaves are so smooth that the rain easily washes all dust and soot from them, and this is why this tree manages to live in a city better than those which have crinkled, or hairy, or sticky leaves, which catch and keep the choking dust.

In most trees the leaf buds are to be found growing between the base of the leaf stem and the twig which supports it. You will find no trace of such buds in the Oriental Plane; they are carefully hidden, and are tenderly protected in a marvellous way.

You see that the base of the leaf stalk is considerably swollen, and that round it there is a line? If you gently pull the leaf, it will come apart from the twig at this line, and then you will discover that the swollen part of the leaf stalk is hollow, and is fitted like a cap over the tiny leaf bud, which is cosily sheltered within. This baby leaf bud is very sensitive to cold, and has many wrappings as well as the leaf cap. Its outer case is lined with sticky gum, which keeps out any damp; then come many small scales covered with soft fur, and inside these lie the tiny leaves, wrapped in a quilt of soft, silky down. This silky down is golden-brown in colour, and it remains on the young leaf till it is quite grown up. Sometimes the young buds are tempted by bright sunshine to throw off their winter coverings too soon. Then if biting frost comes they all die, and the tree will bear no more buds that year. The Plane tree gets its name from a Greek word which means a shield, and this name was given because its broad, flat leaves cast a very welcome shade in hot Eastern lands.

In winter it is easy to recognise the Oriental Plane by its curious seeds. Hanging on the bare branches are strings of round bristly fruit balls (5), three or four, or even five, threaded like large beads on a long slender chain. There are no seed balls such as these on the Sycamore tree, nor on its cousin the Field Maple.

These seed balls are very interesting. Early in spring you see them dangling in the air, and you must pluck one of the green chains and examine its round beads. In one ball are grouped together bunches of purple stamens (3), which have a few pointed, dry scales at the base of each group. As soon as these stamens are ripe and their pollen dust has been blown away, these balls shrivel and fall off. But close beside them, on a similar green chain, are dangling the seed balls (4). Inside these balls there is a soft green cushion, and all over this cushion are stuck small green seeds shaped like pears, each with a tiny point like a stalk standing up at the top. After the stamen dust has fallen on these seeds they enlarge into a small hard nut, and a tuft of bristly down grows up from the base of each seed. The ball becomes a dark brown colour, and it dangles all winter on the tree ; then in spring, when the leaves are ready to burst their coverings, these brown balls fall to the ground and the dry seeds are blown away, each seed floating in the air by the aid of its bristly down.

In America these Eastern and Western Plane trees are called Button trees, because the seed balls resemble old-fashioned buttons.

The wood of the Oriental Plane is used by piano-makers, coach-builders, and cabinet-makers. It is a light brown colour, and is said to be very tough.

PLATE XIII

THE WHITE POPLAR OR ABELE TREE

In the old Greek legends we read that Hercules won a victory over Kakos on Mount Aventine. On the mountain grew a thick grove of Poplar trees, and Hercules, overjoyed with his triumph, bound a branch of the graceful leaves around his brow as a sign of victory. Soon afterwards he went down into the infernal regions, the place of tears and gloom, and when he came back to earth it was seen that the upper side of his leafy garland was darkened with the smoke of Hades, but that the under-side of the leaves had been washed silver white with the sweat which streamed from his brow. Ever since that day the leaves of the Aventine Poplar grow white on the underside, and in course of time its seeds were brought by travellers to Britain, and the tree has taken kindly to our less sunny land. So the tale runs.

It is by these dark green leaves with their thick white lining that you will always know the White Poplar or Abele tree (1), and when you learn how many relations it has, and how closely they resemble each other, you will be glad to have this marked distinction by which you may easily know this member of the family.

The Poplar, like the Willows, prefers to grow in damp places. The most perfect trees are found in meadows close to a river. In France the people plant them along the river banks, and from far away you can trace the windings of the water by the tall Poplar spires which edge its banks.

The Poplars are very fast-growing trees; they will shoot up to a great height in the life-time of a man, and for this reason they are often planted where a screen is quickly required. The lower part of the trunk is dark and is deeply furrowed, but the upper is a dingy yellow colour, and on it there are many black streaks.

Early in March the White Poplar begins to flower. It is one of the catkin-bearing trees, and high on the upper branches there dance and

H

dangle long slender woolly tails of a purplish red colour. These are the stamen catkins (4), and you must pick one to pieces and see how beautifully it is made.

The stamens are grouped together in little bunches of from eight to thirty on a round disc, and at the foot of this disc, on one side, rises a scale which is green on the lower half and reddish brown on the upper half. This scale is deeply and irregularly toothed all round the edge, and is surrounded with fine silk which stands up like a fan. These bunches of stamens are placed all round the catkin tail, with the scales nearly covering the purple stamen heads. As soon as the pollen dust in the stamen heads is ripe and the wind has shaken it out of their dust-bags, the catkin shrivels and falls to the ground. You will find the ground strewn with them in early spring.

But the White Poplar has another catkin flower which bears the seeds, and this flower grows on a separate tree. These seed catkins (3) are stouter and shorter, and are not nearly so noticeable as the long stamen catkins. The green seed-vessel sits in a tiny cup, and on the top of the seed you see a cross of four yellow rays. On one side of the cup rises a scale which is brown at the upper edge and is fringed with down as in the stamen catkin. The wind brings the stamen dust to the four yellow rays on the top of the little seed-vessel, but if there should be no stamen-bearing trees growing near, then the White Poplar can produce no new seeds; it remains barren.

The leaves (2) of the White Poplar are triangular in shape and are deeply jagged all round. When in bud the sides of the leaf are rolled towards the centre, so that the under-side of the leaf, with its thick white lining, is turned outward. The young branches and buds are also thickly covered with fine white down.

The Poplar leaves never seem to be still; they dance and sparkle in the sunshine, and even on quiet days you will see them fluttering. In autumn these leaves turn golden yellow before they fall.

The wood of the White Poplar is too quickly grown to be very durable. It is largely used for making children's toys, because it does not readily split when nails are driven into it. It will not burn easily, and for this reason it makes good floors for dwelling-houses.

Besides the White Poplar or Abele tree there are two other Poplars which are fairly common in this country. One is the Lombardy Poplar, which grows tall and slender like a church spire; its branches rise upward like the flame of a torch, and the tree trunk is clothed to the very ground with withered branches, which never spread outwards, but grow close to the main stem. There is no difficulty in recognising the Lombardy Poplar.

The Black Poplar is also common in many parts of Britain. Its leaves are not lined with white; they are heart-shaped, with no jagged edges, but with dainty little teeth cut evenly all round. The heads of the stamens, which grow in groups on the catkin tail, are very dark purple, and they hang from the end of twigs, which are rough with the scars of last year's leaves.

PLATE XIV

THE ASPEN

"Variable as the shade
By the light, quivering aspen made."
—Scott.

The Aspen (1) is a member of the Poplar family, and in many ways it resembles its cousins. But you will always know an Aspen tree by its leaves (2). These are never still unless when a storm is brooding and the air is perfectly calm; at all other times they shake and quiver incessantly, and you can hear the gentle rustle they make as each leaf rubs against its neighbour. In the Scottish Highlands the country people tell you that the Aspen trembles because at the Crucifixion the cross of Christ was made of Aspen, and the tree must always shudder at the recollection of the cruel purpose it served.

The Aspen is usually found growing in copses,

PLATE XIV

THE ASPEN

1. Aspen Tree   2. Leaf Spray   3. Stamen Catkins   4. Seed Catkin

PLATE XV

THE WHITE WILLOW

1. White Willow Tree   2. Leaf Spray   3. Pussy Buds
4. Stamen Catkin   5. Seed Catkin

or in meadow lands, where it flourishes best in a damp soil; but it is also found on mountain ground, and is very common in the north of Scotland. It is not a long-lived tree: the heart of it begins to decay after fifty or sixty years, just at the age when many of our most familiar trees are at their finest. The wood is very soft, and is of little use either for building or for manufacturing purposes; but it is beautifully white, and sculptors use it for decorative carving; also many of the wooden blocks required by engravers for printing are made of Aspen wood.

The Aspen is one of our catkin-bearing trees. Early in spring you will see dangling on the branches long fluffy tails, which you must pluck and examine carefully. There are two kinds of flowering catkins on the Aspen, and both kinds may be found growing on the same tree. Sometimes you find them close beside each other on the same branch.

In the stamen catkin (3) you see many bunches of tiny stamens with bluey-purple heads: these bunches are dotted all over the catkin tail, and each stamen bunch is nearly hidden by a large scale which rises at one side. This scale is green in the lower half and pale brown in the upper half, and its edges are cut into deep jagged points. This jagged scale lies above the stamen bunch, so that you can just see their heads appearing under the torn edge of the scale. Each stamen is surrounded by a mass of soft grey woolly down, which makes all the catkin look fluffy and silky.

The seed catkin (4) of the Aspen looks much the same as the stamen catkin; it is a long, dangling fat tail, covered with fluffy grey down; but it has no stamens. This catkin bears the seed-vessels, and each seed-vessel resembles a small green pea sitting in a tiny green cup. This pea splits open at the top, and you see four pale pink points rising from the opening. These points are waiting for the stamen dust to reach them, and as soon as that happens they shrivel and disappear; then the seed busies itself in preparing the new plant. Above each green seed-vessel there stands a scale with the edge cut into large torn-looking points. These scales nearly cover the seed-vessel, and they look like brown splashes on the bed of soft fluffy down.

When the seeds are ripe the catkins fall from the tree; the seeds separate from the tail, and the wind blows them a long distance by the aid of the fluffy down which surrounds each seed.

The Aspen leaves (2) are very dainty and pretty. Each leaf grows at the end of a long slender stalk which is flattened like a ribbon, and is placed edge-ways to the twig. The stalk is not strong enough to hold the leaf upright, so it droops, unless when the breeze lifts it in the air, and then you hear a constant rustle-rustle, as if the leaves were whispering to each other. These Aspen leaves are nearly round, and they have evenly-cut teeth on the edges. They are rather small and are dark in colour, and there is no white lining underneath except the soft down which you often find on very young leaves, and which soon disappears.

Through the grass beside its root the Aspen sends up a great many young shoots which are called suckers. The leaves on these young suckers are heart-shaped, and the edges are quite smooth, without any teeth.

Cattle are very fond of these young leaves, so are deer, and goats, and even the beaver. In some places people strip the Aspen leaves from the trees and give them to the cattle, which eat them greedily.

PLATE XV

THE WHITE WILLOW

To distinguish different members of the Willow family is very difficult. It contains many brothers and sisters who are so much alike that you would require to study nothing but willows for many a day if you wished to know each from the other.

In this book are described three different Willows. The first is a lofty tree with a thick trunk and spreading branches; the second is usually a bushy mass of slender twigs bending over the river bed; and the third is a small creeping shrub which twines itself among the roots of the heather, and carpets the ground with masses of silky down. And I think if you know well these three kinds of Willow, you should be able to group the other members of the family around them.

The White Willow (1) is the name given to the largest Willow tree, and very beautiful it is in early spring when the leaves unfold. It has a thick trunk covered with rough, rugged bark, and it sends out large branches, from which grow many smooth, slender twigs. The leaves (2) appear about the middle of May, long narrow leaves which taper to a point, and from a distance you would think that the edges were quite smooth. But when you pick a leaf you find that there are dainty little teeth cut all round the edge. These narrow leaves are covered on both sides with a silky grey down; this gives them a pale, silvery-grey colour, and from a distance you can easily recognise a White Willow tree by the glistening of this beautiful grey foliage, so different from the vivid young green of the Larch and the yellow-green of the Limes and Sycamores.

The White Willow produces two kinds of flowers, and these grow in catkins on different trees. The stamen catkins are the prettiest, and they appear about the same time as the

PLATE XVI

THE GOAT WILLOW

1. Goat Willow or Sallow Tree   2. Leaf Spray   3. Pussy Buds
4. Stamen Catkins   5. Seed Catkins

young leaves. At first these stamen catkins are small egg-shaped buds, closely covered with silky grey down—pussy buds (3) the children call them ; but they open very quickly, and in a few days you will see, dropping from the branches, small green catkins which curl slightly like caterpillars. Each catkin is covered with closely-shut scales, and by the time the leaves are out the scales of these stamen catkins unclose (4). Behind each scale there rises a pair of stamens on long slender stalks. These stamen stalks are hairy on the lower half, and so are the catkin scales. The heads of the stamens are sometimes tinged with red, and between each pair of stamens there lies a honey bag. Notice how constantly the bees are heard buzzing among the Willow branches. When the stamen heads are ripe they burst open, and the fine dust inside is carried by the wind to a Willow tree, on which the seed catkins grow.

These seed catkins (5) are covered with greenish scales, which are tightly pressed together at first. But in the warm spring sunshine the scales unclose, and from the foot of each scale rises a small green pear-shaped seed-vessel which has two tiny straps standing up at the top. The wind wafts the stamen dust to the tree, and some of it falls on these two small straps, which act as messengers and carry the dust down to the inside of the seed-vessel, where the plant makes ready the new seed. Unless you have a seed-bearing

I

tree and a stamen-bearing tree growing within reach of each other, you cannot have any new seeds; but it is possible to increase the number of Willow trees by cutting off branches and planting them in a particular way in the ground, when they will send out roots and grow.

There are two other kinds of White Willow which are found nearly as frequently as the one I have just described, and neither is difficult to recognise. The Golden Willow is the name usually given to one, on account of its twigs, which are a bright shade of yellow-green, and these golden twigs are very noticeable in winter beside the dark branches of the Elms and Beeches. In this Willow the stamens and scales of the dust-producing catkins are the colour of a canary's feathers, and in the spring sunshine they glisten like gold. This is the loveliest of all the Willow trees.

The third White Willow is known as the Crack Willow, because the branches are very easily broken; a knock will snap them from the tree trunk. If ever you try to gather a twig from other Willow trees, you will find how difficult it is to separate it from the branch. The thin green peel, with the leaves clinging to it, comes away in your hand, leaving the bare white twig still clinging to the branch, and without a knife you will scarcely force them apart. But the twigs of the Crack Willow may be snapped across easily, and the large branches are readily broken on a windy night.

The wood of the White and of the Golden Willow is valuable, and is much used by builders for floors and rafters. Coopers say it makes excellent casks, and many of our best cricket bats are made from Willow wood. When straw is scarce people are said to make hats from Willow sprays. They gather the small branches and split them into long, thin strips, and these are woven into fine plaits, which are then joined together.

PLATE XVI

THE GOAT WILLOW OR SALLOW

" In Rome upon Palm Sunday
    They bear true palms,
The cardinals bow reverently
    And sing old psalms.

Elsewhere these psalms are sung
    Beneath the olive branches,
The holly-bush supplies their place
    Amid the avalanches."

The second Willow or group of Willows you should learn about is the most difficult of all. In it there are many different varieties, and you would require to plant one of each kind in your garden, as a gentleman in England has done, and study them carefully for many years to discover the points wherein each Willow differs from the other.

Though the Goat Willow or Sallow (1) sometimes grows into a tall tree, it is more often seen as a bush—a bush with a short, rough stem, which does not rise far above the ground, and which sends up many tall, slender branches, covered with smooth, purplish brown peel or skin. Early in March, before the snowdrops have withered, you will find the Goat Willow in every hedge and coppice bursting into scaly brown buds. It is one of our earliest trees, and after a few days of warm sunshine the brown scales unclose and the branches are dotted with the softest and silkiest little pussy buds (3), shaped like tiny eggs and covered with grey down.

These buds grow alternately on the smooth stem with a small space between each bud. In a few days the baby buds have changed, and you may find two Willow bushes growing quite near each other on which the buds are very different. For those woolly buds are the flower catkins, and the Goat Willow bears two kinds of flowers, which do not grow on the same tree.

The bees have found out that the Willow is in flower; you can hear a swarm of them buzzing in the leafless branches, and you wonder where there is any honey to be found. On one tree the soft grey downy buds have grown larger, and they are now golden yellow catkins (4). The whole bud is covered with dainty yellow-headed stamens, nestling in pairs among oval scales edged with silky down, and it is at the base of these yellow-headed stamens that the bee finds the sweet drops of honey juice.

For many hundreds of years branches of the Goat Willow or Sallow have been carried in this country to church on Palm Sunday in remembrance of the branches of palm which the people strewed in front of Christ when He entered Jerusalem. Troops of boys and girls go into the country lanes and coppices to gather Willow-palms, which they sometimes pluck so roughly and carelessly that the tree remains broken and ruined for the rest of the year. These silky stamen catkins of the Goat Willow are one of the most welcome signs of the return of spring.

But there are other Willow flowers to be looked at: flowers which may not be so attractive, but which bear the seeds and make ready the new plants. These flowers are silky too, and underneath the soft down is an egg-shaped catkin (5), covered with small pear-shaped green seeds. Each seed has a thick yellow point at the top, and at the base there rises a scale which is pointed like a cat's ear and is covered with long, silky hairs. When the stamen flowers are ripe their yellow heads burst, and the fine dust which fills them falls on the backs of the bees who are sipping the honey juice. Then they fly

away to find another honey flower, and they
often alight on a seed catkin, where the pollen
dust is shaken off among the little yellow points
which are waiting for it to help in the making of
the new seeds. Each flower catkin sits upright
on a tuft of small pale green leaves.

The leaves (2) of the Goat Willow are very
different from those of the other Willows; they
are broad and oval, with edges which are crinkled
or waved all round and with a network of fine
veins covering the leaf. These leaves, when they
first come out, are covered with white down,
but by the time they are full grown they are
dark and shiny on the upper side, and are only
downy beneath.

There is another bushy Willow which perhaps
you might mistake for the Goat Willow or Sallow:
this is the Purple Osier. It grows in boggy
marshes, by the banks of slow-running streams,
and it too has silky grey catkins. But you will
easily recognise the Purple Osier by two things.
It has long, slender stems like whips, rising
straight from the tree trunk. These slender
stems are covered with a fine purple skin or peel,
and if you try to pick an Osier stem the peel comes
away in your hand, leaving the white Willow stem
still growing. These Osier stems are valuable for
making baskets, and are grown in great quantities
for this purpose.

The second point in which the Purple Osier

differs from the Goat Willow is this: if you gather a yellow catkin and look at the yellow-headed stamens which cover it, you will see that the slender stalks of the stamens are joined together, making one stalk with two yellow heads, whereas in the Goat Willow or Sallow each yellow stamen head sways at the end of its own stalk.

There is one other Willow tree I should like to tell you about, because it is so curious. It is a tree which creeps close to the ground, and which is found growing in great quantities in the Highlands among the grass and heather. It is called the Dwarf Willow, and it too has silky catkins which grow on the tough wiry branches.

You might not notice these stamen catkins, but you could not help noticing the seed catkins. These cover the ground with tufts of white cotton wool like thistle-down, and when you lift one of these tufts you find that the pear-shaped green seed-vessels have split down the centre to allow many tiny seeds to escape, and each seed is winged with a tuft of silky down. After all the seeds have flown away on the wind, the withered seed-vessels still remain on the catkin, no longer green, but a rusty red-brown colour, which is very noticeable among the small glossy green leaves.

PLATE XVII

THE SCOTCH PINE OR SCOTCH FIR

The Scotch Pine (1), or, as it is often called by
mistake, the Scotch Fir, is one of our noblest
trees; it is tall, and rugged, and sturdy, with a
beauty which lies in its strength and dignity rather
than in its grace. In bygone days large tracts
of Scotland were clothed with vast forests of
Scotch Pine, under whose gloomy branches many
wolves roamed and the wild deer wandered in
herds. But the owners of these noble forests cut
down the trees to get money for the timber, and
the wolves have disappeared. There is now only
a scanty remnant of the great army of Pine trees
which once clothed the northern lands of Britain.

Those vast forests were not planted by man.
The young trees sprang from seeds which had
fallen from the woody fruit cones, and were
carried by rooks or other birds to places where
human beings rarely trod. There the young
seeds grew and sent out their greedy roots. If
the soil was good and plentiful they produced a
strong carrot-shaped root, which bored deep into
the ground and gave the tree such a firm hold
that no storm could tear it up. But if the ground
had only a little earth on the surface and there
were hard rocks beneath, then the roots crept
like serpents near the surface of the soil, clasping
the rocks with a tight grip to steady the tree.

PLATE XVII

THE SCOTCH PINE

1. Scotch Pine Tree 2. Leaf Needles 3. Stamen Flower
4. Seed Flower (pink cones) 5. Green Cones 6. Grey Cone
7. Seed with Wing

How the wind roars in the Pine branches on the high mountain lands! It is like the sound of the sea. If the Pine tree had broad leaves, such as the Sycamore or the Lime tree, it would soon be blown down; but the storm gusts pass through its fine needle-leaves, and no harm is done.

The trunk of the Scotch Pine is very rough, and it is covered with rugged pieces of reddish bark, separated from each other by deep furrows. It rises to a great height, throwing out many large branches on each side, and there is always a bushy rounded tree-top looking up to the sky. In a Pine forest the lower part of the tree is usually bare. This is because the trees are planted so close together there is little air except near the top of the tree, and the lower branches are stifled.

Beneath the branches the ground is always carpeted with fallen Pine leaves, and very curious these Pine leaves (2) are. They look like green needles with soft blunt points, and the edges of each needle are rolled back so that the leaf appears round above and is boat-shaped below. The under-side of the needle is much lighter in colour than the dark green surface.

These needle-leaves usually grow in pairs, though you may find a bunch containing three or even four needles; they are held together by a thin grey sheath, which looks like paper and

K

clasps the end of the bunch. These needle-bunches are placed all round the twig, close to-gether, so as to form a dense brush. They remain on the tree for two or three years, then they fall; but their work is not done. Very often the Pine tree seed has been carried to some sandy seashore upon which nothing is willing to grow. There it takes root and flourishes, and in course of time it throws down handfuls of withered needle-leaves on the loose sandy ground. These needles decay and form a bed of soil which binds the sand together, and when the wind and the birds bring other seeds, they find a place in which they can take root and grow. In France great tracts of waste land have become valuable in this way through the planting of Pine trees.

The Pine tree has its flowers in catkins and its fruit in cones. The catkins are of two kinds, and they grow on the same tree, sometimes on the same branch. The stamen flowers (3) are found in dense spikes at the end of last year's bushy twig. They look like a cluster of bunches of small yellow grains from which a tuft of fine green spears rises in the centre. These grains are the stamen heads, and in May and June they send out clouds of fine yellow powder, which floats in the air and settles on the leaves and on the grass and on the margins of lakes and rivers, where you can see little patches of it lying. Country peasants sometimes tell you that this yellow powder is sulphur which has fallen from the sky during a thunder-storm!

The seed flowers (4) of the Pine tree are very different. They grow either singly or in pairs at the end of this year's new twig, and at first they are tiny pale pink cones. These cones are egg-shaped, and are made up of scales tightly pressed together, with little hard dots showing at the tip of each scale. The seeds are behind the scales, but you will not see them for a long time, as the cone takes eighteen months to grow up. At the end of the first summer you find that the pink cone has become a rich green colour (5) and is still soft, but when the second summer comes round, the cone is ash-grey in colour (6) and is hard and woody.

When the seeds are ripe the tightly-pressed scales unclose and curl up, showing thick wooden lips; at the base of each scale lie two white seeds, and each seed (7) has a thin filmy wing. When the seeds fall from the cone they are blown long distances, floating on the air by their filmy wings.

There is a bird called the cross-bill which is very fond of Pine seeds, and very clever at picking them out of the half-opened cones.

You will occasionally find a tree, very similar to the Scotch Pine, in which the cones grow in groups of three or four together at the end of the twigs. This tree is called the Cluster Pine, and you will notice that its bunches of leaves are different in colour: they are a bluey green, and the tips of the needles are yellowish, as if they had begun to wither.

The wood of the Pine tree is very valuable. Thousands of pounds were paid for the trees in the old Scotch forests, and many stout ships were built from their sturdy trunks. Besides the good timber, the Pine tree gives us turpentine and resin from its juice. If you cut a hole in a Pine tree stem a thick juice will soon be seen oozing from this hole, and it quickly hardens into a clear gum.

PLATE XVIII

THE YEW

Once upon a time a discontented Yew tree grew in a country graveyard. Other trees, it thought, had larger and more beautiful leaves which fluttered in the breeze and became red and brown and yellow in the sunshine, and the Yew tree pined because the fairies had given it such an unattractive dress. One morning the sunshine disclosed that all its green leaves had changed into leaves made of gold, and the heart of the Yew tree danced with happiness. But some robbers, as they stole through the forest, were attracted by the glitter, and they stripped off every golden leaf. Again the tree bemoaned its fate, and next day the sun shone on leaves of purest

PLATE XVIII

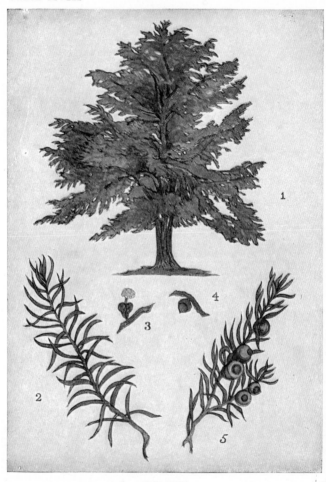

THE YEW

1. Yew Tree   2. Leaf Spray   3. Stamen Flower
4. Seed Flower   5. Spray with Fruit

PLATE XIX

THE JUNIPER

1. Juniper Bushes   2. Leaf Spray with Flowers
3. Stamen Flower (much enlarged)   4. Seed Flower (much enlarged)
5. Spray with Fruit

crystal. "How beautiful!" thought the tree; "see how I sparkle!" But a hailstorm burst from the clouds, and the sparkling leaves lay shivered on the grass. Once more the good fairies tried to comfort the unhappy tree. Smooth broad leaves covered its branches, and the Yew tree flaunted these gay banners in the wind. But, alas, a flock of goats came by and ate of the fresh young leaves "a million and ten." "Give me back again my old dress," sobbed the Yew, "for I see that it was best." And ever since its leaves remain unchanging, and it wears the sombre dress which covered its boughs in the days when King William landed from Normandy on our shores, and the swineherd tended his pigs in the great forests which covered so much of Merry England.

In history books we read how important the Yew tree once was. Long before the invention of guns and gunpowder, many of our soldiers carried bows made of Yew tree wood, and from these they shot deadly arrows with tremendous force. Three of England's Kings—Harold, William Rufus, and Richard Cœur de Lion—were slain by such arrows, and it was from a Yew tree bow that Tell sent the arrow that halved the apple placed on his son's head.

The Yew tree (1) grows very, very slowly; it never becomes a tall tree, not even when it has lived hundreds and hundreds of years, because, instead of sending up one thick trunk, it has the strange habit of dividing into a cluster of trunks, three or four or more of equal thickness, which rise from one root. These trunks are covered with browny red bark and are very smooth; the red bark peels off in thin flakes, and you can see that the wood beneath it is a deep orange red.

From the clustered trunks many branches stretch out to form a densely bushy tree; these branches are closely covered with small twigs, on which grow short narrow leaves (2), ending in blunt points, and with the edges slightly curved backwards. These leaves grow alternately all round the twig, and they are dark and glossy above but much paler beneath. They do not fall from the tree in winter, as the Yew, like the Holly, is one of our evergreen trees. Yew tree leaves are very poisonous, and many tales are told of cattle and horses which have died from eating them.

Some people believe that the Yew tree is planted in churchyards because it is poisonous and is associated with death; while others think just the opposite, and say that it is placed among the tombstones to remind us that the soul is undying, like the Yew tree leaves.

In February or March if you strike a Yew tree bough with a stick you will see clouds of fine yellow powder rising from the tree. This powder is the stamen dust, and if you pull a spray of leaves and examine it you will discover clusters of small oval yellow flowers (3) nestling close to the main stem where the leaf joins it. The Yew tree belongs to the great family of trees whose fruit is a cone and which bear their flowers in catkins. Take a magnifying-glass, and it will show you that each catkin is composed of a bunch of stamens rising from a slender pillar at the foot of which are a few dry, papery scales. Each stamen has six dust-bags at the end, and when the stamen powder is ripe these dust-bags open, and the fine yellow powder is blown like meal over the leaves and seeds.

The Yew tree has seed flowers (4) as well as those which bear the stamens. Usually they grow on a different tree, but occasionally you will find them on the same Yew, but on a separate branch. It is a curious thing about the Yew tree and its relations that these seeds are not covered in any way, but lie naked to the sun and rain. They always grow on the under-side of the stem, and at first they look like tiny acorns. You notice a small disc surrounded by a few scales, and on this disc sits the little green acorn with its olive green skin. This acorn is waiting for the stamen dust to reach it. As soon as the wind has blown the yellow powder over it a beautiful cup of pale pink wax grows round the green seed. There is no hard, woody cone on the Yew tree ; the fruit (5) is this pale

pink waxen berry, shaped like a fairy cup and
filled with sticky juice. The walls of the pink cup
are soft and fleshy, and you can just see the tip of
the green seed standing up in the centre. They
are very lovely, these waxy pink berries on the dark
green spray, but they are said to be poisonous.

Sometimes at the end of a Yew spray there
grows a curious-looking cone like a small artichoke, made of soft green leaves. This is caused
by a tiny gnat which lays its eggs in a Yew tree
bud, and in some strange way that we do not
understand causes it to develop this tuft of
strange leaves. You will remember that in the
Oak a similar growth is found.

The wood of the Yew tree is very hard and
durable, as are all woods which grow slowly.
"A Yew tree post will outlast a post of iron" is a
saying often repeated by farmers; but the Yew
wood is not much in demand for manufacturing
purposes.

PLATE XIX

THE JUNIPER

In the Bible we read that when Elijah fled from
the cruel persecution of King Ahab and the wicked
Queen Jezebel, he sat down under a Juniper tree
to rest. When we look at the Juniper as it grows
in this country, we wonder how the prophet could
have found rest beside such a prickly tree, or shade

beneath such a small one. But in other lands the Juniper grows much taller; and as all books about trees give it a place beside its relations the Yew and the Scotch Pine, it must be included among the common trees you should learn to know.

In Britain the Juniper (1) is found on heathy commons or high on the upland plains, where it flourishes as a large, thick, bushy shrub, and occasionally shoots up into a small tree. It is rather a gloomy-looking tree: in spring time, when most of our trees look fresh and bright in their young green leaves, the Juniper shows little change. Its leaves are evergreen, and the new leaves grow in small tufts at the tips of the branches, so that you scarcely notice them.

The Juniper bark is dark reddish brown, and it flakes off in small pieces in the same way as the Yew tree bark. The branches are small and thin, and they clothe the trunk close to the very ground; it would be difficult to sit comfortably under a Juniper tree in this country. Like the Yew, it is a very slow-growing tree.

Juniper leaves (2) are not in the least like ordinary leaves: they are more like thorns than leaves, and they are not easy to gather. But if you examine a spray carefully you will find that each leaf is like a narrow flat spear with a sharp point at the end. Each leaf has a slight groove cut from end to end in the upper side, which is dark green, very smooth and glossy. Notice how

L

curiously the leaves are grouped on the spray. They are placed in incomplete circles of three, and there is always a short space between each of the circles.

Juniper flowers are of two kinds, and they usually grow on separate trees, though sometimes you may find both kinds on separate branches of the same tree. The stamen flowers (3) are in full bloom in May, and you will find them growing in small scaly catkins close to the foot of the leaf where it joins the stem. The heads of the stamens stand like a row of small yellow beads along the edge of each scale, and when they are ripe the beads burst and the leaves around are covered with their fine yellow powder.

The seed flowers (4) also grow at the foot of the leaves, and at first you might mistake them for young buds. They have thicker and more fleshy scales than those of the stamen catkins, and after the yellow stamen dust is blown by the wind on to their seed-vessels the upper scales grow into a green berry (5). These green berries remain in the tree all through the winter, and the following summer they change into a deep purplish black. Each berry has a soft grey bloom all over it, like the bloom on a grape.

These berries are very bitter to taste, but are not poisonous; in some illnesses country people use them successfully as a medicine.

Many are the uses of the Juniper, and in olden days it was highly valued.

In Sweden the berries are eaten to breakfast; sometimes they are roasted and ground into coffee.

The wood and its berries may be burnt in sick-rooms to purify the air and refresh the patient. Country people believed that burning sprays of Juniper kept away witches, and the smoke was supposed to drive away serpents, as well as to destroy any germs of plague or other infectious disease.

In Scotland the smoke from a Juniper fire is used for curing hams.

In Lapland the peasants make ropes from the Juniper bark, and they tell you that if a bit of Juniper wood is lighted and then carefully covered with ashes it will keep alight for a whole year.

The trunk of the Juniper tree is too small and slight to be very useful as timber; but good walking-sticks are often made from the branches and young stems.

PLATE XX

THE LARCH

" When rosy plumelets tuft the larch."
—Tennyson.

The Larch (1) was brought to Britain in the seventeenth century from its home on the high mountains of Germany, Austria, and Italy. It has taken kindly to our cheerless climate, and now covers acres of what was once barren moorland.

A few years after Larches are planted the long flexible branches of the young trees meet and form a thicket into which little light or air can enter, and the weeds and heather growing round the tree roots are stifled. Each winter the Larch sheds on the bare ground millions of its tiny needle-leaves, which enrich the soil.

After the young trees have grown to a certain height the forester thins the plantation; he cuts down a number of the young trees, so that those which remain may have more room to grow, and he removes all the withered branches near the ground. This allows the sunshine to reach the soil, and soon after a crop of soft, fine grass is seen carpeting the ground. Sheep and cattle can now be pastured where a short time before there grew nothing but heather and weeds.

Look at a Larch plantation in winter-time, and you will think that all the trees are dead. The Pines and the Firs are resting, and the Oaks and Beeches seem asleep, but their branches do not have the dead, withered look of the Larch trees. Come again early in spring, and you will see a wonderful change. These dead twigs are now a pale glossy brown, so glossy that they might have been varnished. Try to pull one, and you will find how tough and sound it is; only where the twig joins the branch can you separate

PLATE XX

THE LARCH

1. Larch Tree
4. Seed Catkins
2. Leaf Tufts
5. Young Cone
3. Stamen Catkins
6. Ripe Cone

PLATE XXI

THE SPRUCE FIR

1. Spruce Fir Tree   2. Leaf Spray   3. Stamen Flowers
4. Seed Flower   5. Cone   6. Seed Scale
7. Growth caused by an Insect

it from the tree; and what a delightful smell of turpentine remains on your fingers after gathering the Larch twigs!

In the trunk of this tree there are stores of turpentine, tiny lakes of it, which are of considerable value. In Italy, where the Larch trees grow to great size, small holes are bored through the trunk to the very heart of the tree, and a thin pipe is put in. Then a can is hung on the end of the pipe, and the pure turpentine juice drops steadily into the can. It is then strained, and is sold just as it comes from the tree.

Early in April the Larch tree begins to get ready for summer; it is always one of the first trees to awaken at the call of spring. On each flexible twig there appear little brown scaly knobs like small beads, placed either singly or in pairs with a short space between each bead. In a few days these scaly beads burst open, and a tuft of vivid green leaves (2), like the fringes round the mouth of a sea-anemone, peeps out. These leaves are soft and flat and slender, very different from the hard needles of the Pine and the harsh swords of the Fir trees, and they grow in tufts, thirty or forty together, rising from the centre of the scaly brown bead. Each tuft is of the brightest green. So the Larch tree is a very vision of spring in the dark Fir plantations, while the leaf buds of many other trees are only awakening from their winter sleep.

In the hedgerows the Hawthorns are in full leaf, the stamen flowers cluster on the boughs of the Elm, and the Hazel and Willow catkins dangle their tails in the wind; but the forest trees remain sombre and gloomy, and the young Larch seems gay as the sunlight among them. As the season advances the Larch tree leaves become darker, and they fall early in winter. We have only one other cone-bearing tree which is not evergreen, and that is the Cypress.

After the leafy tufts appear you will notice that some of the scaly brown beads have not produced any leaves; instead they have become tiny oval catkins (3), which are made up of a crowd of small yellow grains. These catkins are the stamen flowers, and in the yellow grains, which are the heads of the stamens, is prepared the dust powder which the seed flowers require to assist them in getting ready the new seed.

On the same twig, and not far from the stamen catkins, you see a beautiful deep rose-red seed catkin (4). This tiny rose-red catkin is very lovely among the brilliant green tufts of leaves; no other cone-bearing tree has anything so attractive to show us. At first the catkin scales are soft and fleshy; they overlap each other very loosely, and from the base of each scale there rises a bright green point like a single needle-leaf.

In a few weeks the catkin has become a young cone (5), which looks like a small rosy egg sitting erect on a bent footstalk, then the rose-pink colour fades from the cone, and the scales become hard and woody. Behind each scale lie two tiny white seeds with wings, and there is a coating of sticky resin over these seeds to keep them dry. The ripe cones (6) remain on the tree for years, long after the seeds have been blown away on their transparent wings by the wind.

The crossbill often builds his nest in a Larch tree. He is particularly fond of Larch tree seeds, and is very clever at picking them out of the ripe cones.

The trunk of a full-grown Larch is reddish brown in colour, and it is covered with a rough, scaly bark, which is often hung with hoary tufts of pale grey lichen.

Larch wood is very valuable, and is used for many purposes. It is very tough, and does not rot in water. Joiners tell us there are fewer knots in planks of Larch than in those of either Silver Fir or Spruce. Wood knots are scars which occur where a dead branch has fallen from the tree, and builders complain that when the tree is sawn into planks, the knots shrink and fall out, leaving a round hole. This reduces the value of the wood; but in the Larch planks the knots are said not to come away from the surrounding wood.

PLATE XXI

THE SPRUCE FIR

Although the Scotch Pine is sometimes called the Scotch Fir, the latter name is generally admitted to be a mistake. It was given long ago by people who had not seen the real Fir trees, and who did not know how different they are from the Pines. It is several hundred years since the Spruce Fir was brought to this country, but it is not one of our native trees, like the Scotch Pine, the Yew, and the Juniper.

The Spruce (1) is one of our tallest trees; it loves to grow on ground many thousand feet above the level of the sea; and in Switzerland and Norway there are great forests of these slender, soldier-like trees, clothing the sides of the giant snow mountains. With us it does not grow so abundantly, but you will find many Spruce Firs mingling with the Scotch Pine in the large woods of our Scotch Highlands.

The Spruce Fir has a very straggling root which does not penetrate far into the ground; it creeps along close under the surface, and intertwines itself with any other tree roots in the neighbourhood. This does not give it a very firm hold, and after great gales you sometimes find a broad path opened in the Fir woods, which has been made by the Spruce trees falling in the track of the storm.

It is a very straight tree, with a smooth scaly bark of a reddish brown colour; from each side of the trunk slender branches grow straight out like the spokes of a wheel; but each branch rises a little way above the last as the steps rise in a ladder. These branches are very slender, and at first they sweep downwards in graceful curves; but at the tips they all turn upward, so that the points look toward the sky.

The branches get smaller and smaller as the tree grows higher, which gives it the appearance of a pyramid, and at the very top there stands a single upright branch like a spear. This spear-like tip is one of the distinctive features of the Spruce Fir.

The leaves (2) are short and flat and hard, and they are rather prickly to touch. They do not grow in pairs or bundles, as in the Scotch Pine or the Larch; they are placed singly and very close together all round the twig. The twigs grow almost opposite each other on the young sprays, and each spray hangs straight down from the main branch, which looks as if a parting had been made along its centre and the sprays combed evenly to either side. From a distance the Spruce tree branches resemble drooping feathers which curve skyward at the tips.

The Spruce Fir has two kinds of flowers. In May or June, if you look at the tips of the drooping sprays which grew last year, you will see two

M

or three little oval catkins of a pretty yellowish pink colour nestling among the hard, flat leaves. These are the stamen flowers (3), and when ripe they will burst open and scatter a great deal of yellow pollen dust.

The seed flowers (4) grow in cones, and are found at the end of this year's shoots. It is by these cones you will most readily recognise the Spruce Fir. You remember that in the Scotch Pine the full-grown cones were grey and woody, with tightly-pressed lips, and that these lips were very thick and curled upwards when the cone opened?

In the Fir trees the scales of the ripe cones (5) are like thin glossy brown paper. Each scale ends in two sharp little teeth, and the scales are not tightly pressed together, but overlap each other loosely, so that you could put the blade of a knife under each. The woody cones are always found in Pine trees, and the papery cones are characteristic of the Firs.

In the Spruce Fir these cones are about six inches long, with blunt tips, and when full grown they hang from the sprays. Do not forget to notice this, as in some Fir trees the full-grown cones are seated upright on the branches. Under each scale there lie two little seeds (6), with large pale brown wings; these seeds require over a year to ripen, then the wind blows them from the loosened cone scales to many a strange resting-place, where they take root, and a new tree begins to grow.

Sometimes you may see strange leafy-looking bunches (7) like soft, badly-made cones on the young sprays. These are caused by an insect which lays its eggs in the young leaf bud and destroys its graceful shape.

The Spruce Fir has two enemies that do it great harm. These are the crossbill and the squirrel. They break off the young shoots close to the end, and so stop the growth of the branches. You will often find the ground strewn with these fresh green twigs; but you require to sit very still for a long time if you wish to see the enemies at work.

The wood of the Spruce Fir is valuable for many purposes. The tall, smooth tree trunks are used for the masts of ships, for scaffolding poles, and telegraph posts; and many boat-loads of Fir planks are brought from Norway and from the shores of the Baltic Sea, to be manufactured into flooring boards for our houses. In some places the fibre of the Spruce Fir is reduced to pulp, and from this a common kind of paper is produced which is used for newspapers or cheap magazines.

From the sap we get resin and turpentine, and the bark is used in the tanning of leather.

Some people say that the name Fir wood is just a mistake for fire-wood, because in the old days torches were made of the young fir branches, whose gummy twigs burnt easily with a clear, strong light.

PLATE XXII

THE SILVER FIR

Many people find it difficult to distinguish between the Spruce Fir and the Silver Fir, and they are often called by each other's names; yet they are unlike in many points, and a little trouble would prevent such mistakes.

The Silver Fir (1) is not one of our native trees; it was brought from Central or Southern Europe to this country in 1603, and has taken kindly to our moist climate. It does not grow on such lofty mountains as the Spruce, but it will thrive at a level of six thousand feet above the sea, higher than the highest mountain in Great Britain.

It is a tall, stately tree, but it is bushier and less regular than the Spruce Fir. The trunk is covered with greyish brown bark, which is smooth when the tree is young; but as the tree grows old—and the Silver Fir will live for four hundred years—this bark cracks into many rugged fissures. You remember that the Spruce tree has a sharp spear-like point rising from the very top of the trunk. In the Silver Fir the tree is only pointed when very young, and by the time it is full grown the top is bushy, with many small unequal branches standing out from the main stem.

PLATE XXII

THE SILVER FIR

| 1. Silver Fir Tree | 2. Leaf Spray | 3. Stamen Flowers |
| 4. Cone Flower | 5. Ripe Cone | 6. Seed Scale |

PLATE XXIII

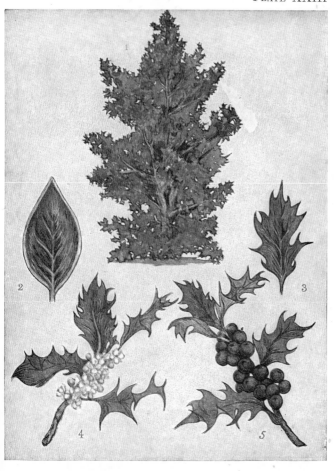

THE HOLLY

1. Holly Tree   2. Blunt Leaf   3. Prickly Leaf

4. Flower Cluster   5. Fruit

These branches do not grow in whorls or circles, like the spokes of a wheel; they are often irregular, and there may be gaps in the tree where a branch has fallen off, and only a scar is left to show where the branch should have been. The Silver Fir is a firmly-rooted tree; it sends a long tap-shaped root, ending in two forks, deep into the soil, so that there is little danger of the wind uprooting it during the wintry gales.

Now look at the leaves (2) which grow on the Silver Fir. Like those of the Spruce, and unlike those of the Pine, they grow singly, each little leaf standing by itself on the rough twig. Although they are placed all round this twig, these leaves have a tendency to grow to right or left of the twig, and look as if they had been parted down the centre and carefully combed to each side.

Each leaf is flat and slender, and on the upper side it is a dark glossy green; the edges are rolled back on to the under-side of the leaf, which is much paler in colour. The centre rib of the leaf is much raised, and looks like a slender cord, and on each side of this cord, between it and the curled-back leaf edge, there runs a silvery white line; it is from this silvery line that the tree gets its name.

Notice that the leaf twigs of the Silver Fir do not droop in the feathery way they do in the Spruce; they are much stiffer, and stand out all round the branch; also, there is not nearly such a marked upward curve at the tip of the branch as you find in the Spruce Fir. The leaves of the Silver Fir remain on the tree eight or nine years, but each year the tree lengthens its sprays, and the young leaves are a beautiful pale yellowish green colour, almost as pale as the young leaves of the primrose.

The stamen flowers (3) grow at the ends of the young sprays. They consist of a few overlapping scales with a cluster of stamens inside. The seed flowers or cones (4) grow on the same tree, sometimes on the same branch, and they become cones in the same way as the seed flowers of the Pine and the Spruce. But you will at once notice a difference. The cones of the Silver Fir grow upright; they sit on the branches with their tops looking up to the sky, whereas the cones of the Spruce and the Scotch Pine when full grown hang down from the ends of the spray with their tips pointing to the ground. If there are any cones visible you will never mistake the Silver Fir for the Spruce.

The ripe cones (5) are made up of many thin, soft scales which overlap each other closely, and each scale ends in a sharp point which turns backward; this gives the cone a hairy appearance. At first the cones are green, like those of the Scotch Pine, but soon they turn purple, and when quite ripe they are a rich red brown.

If the tree is old enough—that means if it is forty years of age—you will find small angular seeds (6), with a long filmy wing attached, nestling behind each scale. But if the tree is still young, the cones are seedless. It takes eighteen months for the cone to ripen, and when the seeds are ready and they and the red-brown scales fall from the cone, a bare brown stick is left standing upright on the branch.

The wood of the Silver Fir is very valuable, and it is used for many purposes; doors and window-frames and floors are constantly made of it, and for shipbuilding it is in great demand. In Switzerland there are great forests of Silver Fir, but they grow high on the mountain sides, where there are no roads and no means of getting the trees brought down after they are felled.

But at Lucerne, a town on the shores of a large lake, with great forests on the mountains above, the people invented an excellent way of overcoming this difficulty.

A narrow avenue was cut in the forest among the trees, and this was floored with trunks of Fir and Spruce. Snow and water were poured down this avenue, which the cold air quickly froze, and the avenue became a gigantic ice-slide eight miles long. The Fir trees were felled, and all their branches lopped off, the bare trunks were placed on this slide, and in six minutes they shot into the waters of the lake eight miles below. There they floated till the wood merchant was ready for them.

The Silver Fir tree is rich in gummy juice, which is made into turpentine and resin. Have you ever seen necklaces of pale cloudy beads, and of clear dark brown made of amber? People tell us this amber is found on the shores of the Baltic Sea, and that it is just the gummy juice which dropped long ago from some kind of Fir tree and has hardened in a mysterious way of which we know nothing.

PLATE XXIII

THE HOLLY

"Below, a circling fence, its leaves are seen, wrinkled and keen.
  No grazing cattle through their prickly round can reach to
      wound;
  But as they grow where nothing is to fear,
  Smooth and unarmed the pointless leaves appear."

—Southey.

The Holly (1) is our most important evergreen, and is so well known that it scarcely needs any description. It has flourished in this country as long as the Oak, and is often found growing under tall trees in the crowded forests, as well as in the open glades, where lawns of fine grass are to be found.

People say that the Holly, or Holm tree, as it is often called, is the greenwood tree spoken of by Shakespeare, and that under its bushy shelter Robin Hood and his merry men held their meetings

PLATE XXIV

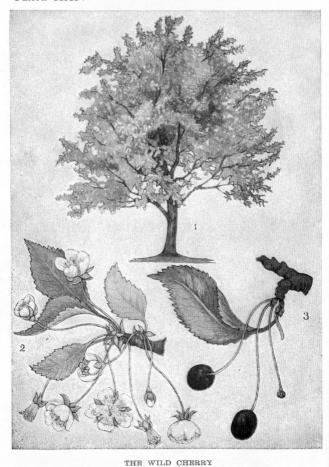

THE WILD CHERRY

1. Wild Cherry or Gean in Autumn   2. Flower Cluster with Leaves
3. Fruit

in the open glades of Sherwood Forest. Sometimes it is called the Holy tree, because from the oldest time of which we have any record its boughs have been used to deck our shrines and churches, and in some parts of England the country people in December speak of gathering Christmas, which is the name they give to the Holly, or Holy tree. It is this evergreen which we oftenest use at Christmas-tide to decorate our churches, and very lovely the dark green sprays, with their coral berries, look when twined round the grey stone pillars.

The Holly is looked upon as a second-rate forest tree. It is never very large, and it usually appears as a thick, tall bush, with many branches reaching almost to the ground. Sometimes you find it with a slender, bare trunk, clothed with pale grey bark, and if you look closely at this bark you will see that it is covered with curious black markings, as if some strange writing had been traced on it with a heavy black pen.

This writing is the work of a tiny plant which makes its home on the Holly stem and spreads in this strange way.

The bark of the young Holly shoots and boughs is pale green and quite smooth.

The tree requires little sunshine, and it seems to keep all it gets, as every leaf is highly polished and reflects the light like a mirror. These leaves grow closely on every branch; they are placed

N

alternately on each side of the twigs, and are oval, with the edges so much waved that the leaves will not lie flat, but curl on each side of the centre rib.

The prickly leaves (3) which grow low down on the tree have sharp spines along the waved edges, and a very sharp spine always grows at the point of the leaf. But the upper branches are clothed with blunt leaves (2) which have no spines along the edges; instead there is a pale yellow line round each leaf, and there is a single blunt spine at the point.

Sheep and deer are very fond of eating the tough, leathery leaves of the Holly, and it is believed that the tree clothes its lower branches in prickly leaves to protect itself from these greedy enemies.

Country people tell you that if branches of smooth Holly are the first to be brought into the house at Christmas-time, then the wife will be head of the house all the next year, but if the prickly boughs enter first, then the husband will be ruler.

The Holly leaves hang on the tree several years, and after they fall they lie a long time on the ground before the damp soaks through their leathery skin and makes them decay. You will find Holly leaves from which all the green part of the leaf has disappeared, leaving a beautiful skeleton leaf of grey fibre, which is still perfect in every vein and rib.

The flowers (4) of the Holly bloom in May.

They appear in small crowded clusters between the leaf stalk and the twig, and each flower is a delicate pale pink on the outside, but is pure white within. There is a calyx cup edged with four green points, and inside this cup stands a long white tube, with four white petals at the top. There are four yellow-headed stamens, and a tiny seed-vessel is hidden inside the flower tube. Sometimes all these parts will be found complete in a single flower; sometimes there will be flowers on the same branch which have stamens and no seed-vessel, and others which have seed-vessels and no stamens. Perhaps you will find a whole tree on which not a single seed flower grows. This tree may be laden with lovely white flowers in spring, but it will bear no berries in winter. You must have both stamen flowers and seed flowers if the tree is to produce any fruit.

As summer passes, the seed-vessels, which have had stamen dust scattered over them, become small green berries (5), and these berries turn yellow and then change into a deep red, the colour of coral or sealing-wax. The berries cluster round the green stalk, and most beautiful they are among the glossy dark leaves. Inside each berry there are four little fruit stones containing seeds, and the birds love to eat these red berries, which are full of mealy pulp; but remember that children must never eat the Holly berries, as they are poisonous except for the birds.

You will find that if the Holly tree has a good
crop of berries this winter there will not be many
the following year; the tree seems to require a
year's rest before it can produce a second large
crop.

There are some Holly trees with leaves which
are shaded with pale yellow or white—variegated
Hollies, we call them. These are greatly prized
for planting in gardens, where the bushes with
different-coloured leaves lend much beauty when
all the trees are bare in winter.

The wood of the Holly is too small to be of
much use. It is white and very hard, and when
stained black it is largely used instead of ebony,
which is scarce and expensive. The black
handles of many of our silver teapots are made of
stained Holly wood. A sticky lime, which is used
for snaring birds, is made from the young green
shoots and twigs, and the slender branches are
good for making walking-sticks and coachmen's
whips.

PLATE XXIV

THE WILD CHERRY OR GEAN

There are now more than forty varieties of
Cherry in Britain, and they all are descended from
the Gean or Wild Cherry tree. This favourite
tree belongs to the great Rose family, and is

related to the Apple, and Pear, and Plum. It grows freely all over Britain except in the very north of Scotland; and we read that six hundred years ago the county of Kent was famous for its Cherry orchards.

In Germany the Cherry is planted for many miles by the roadsides, so that all passers-by may eat the fruit and enjoy the shade cast by the tall trees. And if there should be any particular tree whose fruit the owner does not wish taken, he ties a wisp of straw round that tree, and the people understand the sign and do not touch these Cherries.

In France the Wild Cherry fruit, along with a little bread and butter, is often the only food of the poor charcoal-burners and wood-cutters, who stay in the forest during the cold winter months.

Song birds, especially the blackbirds, love to eat cherries, and as we are very grateful to the birds for eating the many grubs and insects which destroy our fruit and corn, we must not grudge them a feast from our Cherry trees. It is probably the birds who have carried the seeds to the many different places where we find Cherry trees spring-ing up.

The Wild Cherry (1) is a tall tree with wide-spreading branches. It has a smooth grey bark, from which you will often see oozing large drops of clear gum. This gum is very sticky, it will not melt in cold water, and it is very difficult to

remove from your fingers. The Wild Cherry
leaves (2) appear in spring, long oval leaves ending
in a point, and with sharp teeth along the edge.
These leaves are very soft, and they droop from
the twigs. At first the leaf is folded lengthways,
with the two edges meeting, and it is a dull brown
colour; but this colour soon changes in the sunshine to a soft green, and when autumn comes
you find leaves of every shade of pink and red
and crimson.

The large white Cherry blossoms (2) come
almost at the same time as the leaves, and they
grow in loose clusters, in which the flowers hang
from the end of long, drooping stalks. There are
always many small leaf-like scales where these
flower stalks join the twig. Each blossom has
a pear-shaped calyx at the end of the flower stalk,
and this calyx is edged with five green points.
These points fold back against the stalk after
the flower is withered.

There are five large snowy petals which make
the flower clusters look very lovely in the spring
sunshine, but the petals fall very quickly and
strew the ground with their snowy flakes.

Within the petal circle there are many slender
stamens, and you can see a long red-tipped point
rising from the seed-vessel, which lies concealed
in the pear-shaped calyx which stands beneath
the petals and sepals.

The Wild Cherry fruit (3) is black, and sometimes

dark red. It is rather sour, and the cherries we buy in the shops are usually cherries which have been cultivated in an orchard, and have been grown in a warmer country.

In Cambridgeshire there is a festival called Cherry Sunday, when every one goes to the Cherry orchard, and on paying sixpence may eat as many cherries as he pleases.

For some unknown reason the cuckoo has always been associated with the Cherry tree. There is an old proverb which says, "The cuckoo never sings till he has thrice eaten his fill of cherries"; and country children play a delightful game in which he has a part. They join hands and dance round a Cherry tree, singing—

> "Cuckoo, Cherry tree,
> Come down and tell to me,
> How many years I have to live."

Then each child shakes one of the Cherry tree branches, and the number of cherries that fall tell him how many years he will live. If five cherries fall he has five years to live, and if twelve cherries fall he will live twelve years, and so on.

There is a cunning little bird called the woodpecker which very often visits the Cherry tree. He eats the insects that live on its bark; and you can hear his bill peck, pecking at the trunk as he picks up his food.

The wood of the Cherry tree is hard, yet easily

worked. It is much in demand by furniture makers, and is a rich red colour which can be highly polished.

PLATE XXV

THE WHITEBEAM

In the old Saxon language, which was once the language spoken by most of the people in England, the word beam means a tree, so we must be careful not to speak of the Whitebeam tree, as that would be just the same as to say the White tree tree.

The Whitebeam (1) is not nearly so common as the Oak, or the Ash or Beech, and yet it has been known in this country for many hundred years. It is found growing stiff and tall on bleak chalky pastures as well as in beautiful parks and plantations. The trunk is covered with a rough brown bark, and there are great deep roots which spread widely and keep the tree firmly attached to the soil.

It is easy to see why this tree is called the Whitebeam. Look at the fat buds which have been on the tree all winter, making you think that spring was close at hand. In April these buds burst open, and you see that the young leaves inside are covered with a thick coating of woolly down. They are the woolliest buds which grow in this country, and the leaves (2), when they first

PLATE XXV

THE WHITEBEAM

1. Whitebeam   2. Flower Cluster with Leaves   3. Fruit Cluster with Leaves

come out, are as white as if they had been sprinkled with flour. They are pretty leaves, broad and oval, with large teeth cut all round the edge and with clearly-marked veins. At first each leaf is white above as well as below, but as it gets older the woolly down disappears from the upper side, and the leaf becomes a dark, glossy green. But watch the tree some day when the wind is stirring, and at every gust the dark green leaves blow upwards and sideways, and you will see that the back of each leaf is silvery white— the woolly lining has remained. You remember that the white Poplar or Abele tree had leaves which were white-lined too.

The flowers of the Whitebeam (2) resemble those of the Rowan, but they are larger and are not so closely clustered together on their short stalks. Each flower has five pointed green sepals standing out like the rays of a star beneath the circle of five white petals. There is a ring of delicate stamens with yellow heads within the petal circle, and the seeds are concealed in the pear-shaped swelling which supports the flower at the end of the flower stalk. There are often dark spots on the main flower stem from which all the smaller ones branch.

After the white petals and the stamens have fallen off, the swollen flower stalk enlarges and becomes an oval berry (3), considerably larger than that of the Rowan. At first the berries are

o

covered with white down, but soon that wears off, and you see that the berries are smooth and are a rich red colour. They are not good to eat, these attractive-looking berries, though people say they are pleasant when over-ripe and ready to decay. But the birds love them, and so do hedgehogs and squirrels.

In France the people plant a great many White-beams. This is because the small birds require the berries for food in the winter, when there are no longer grubs and insects to be found. These grubs and insects destroy the vines and corn when they are young and tender in early spring, and the small birds are needed because they eat these pests, and so save the young plants.

The wood of the Whitebeam is not much used, though small objects, such as wooden spoons, knife handles, and combs, are made of it. It is very hard, and will take a high polish.

PLATE XXVI

THE ROWAN OR MOUNTAIN ASH

"Their spells were vain, the boy returned
    To the Queen in sorrowful mood,
  Crying that witches have no power
    Where there is Roan tree wood."
                                —Old Song.

The Rowan tree is closely related to the roses, and is a cousin of the Hawthorn, the Apple, and the Pear. It is not related in any way to the

Ash, but the leaves have some resemblance, because, like the Ash tree leaves, they are made up of many pairs of small leaflets growing opposite each other on each side of a centre stalk, and with an odd leaflet at the end. But the leaflets of the Ash tree have each a stalk; those in the Rowan have none, and in the Ash tree each large feathery leaf is planted exactly opposite its neighbour, while in the Rowan the leaves grow alternately. The name Mountain Ash is a mistake.

The Rowan tree (1) is seen at its best among the wild glens and mountains of the north and west of Scotland. It requires air and light, and will flourish in almost any kind of soil, and many are the tales which are woven round the life of this beautiful tree. It is called the Roan, or whispering tree, because it has secrets to tell to those who will listen. No witches or evil spirits can cross a door over which a branch of Rowan is nailed, and no harm will happen to him who has a sprig of Rowan pinned to his coat. In every churchyard in Wales a Rowan tree is planted to scare away demons who might disturb the sleep of the dead; and on lonely farms high up on the mountain sides, the Witchin, or Wiggin tree, as it used to be called, is placed close beside the dwelling-house.

The Rowan is not a large tree; it grows easily and requires no pruning, as its branches rarely die, and the tree never loses its graceful shape.

The branches are wiry and slender, and they all point upward. The bark is a dark purple colour and is glossy and smooth; across it there are many curious deep gashes, as if the tree had been scored with a knife.

The Rowan is often planted in new coppices to shield the young trees, but as soon as these grow up and throw out many branches, they stifle their kind nurse, which cannot grow without plenty of light and air.

Early in spring the Rowan buds appear, fat woolly buds covered with grey cottony down. The young leaves (3) are carefully packed inside among plenty of cotton wool, and very downy they look when they first come out. Each leaflet is toothed round the edge, and is dark glossy green above and much paler green underneath. These leaves remain on the tree till late in autumn, then when the frost touches them with its icy fingers they change to wonderful shades of gold and scarlet and pink, and they fall with the October winds.

The Rowan tree flowers (2) blossom in May, and they grow in dense clusters, each flower at the end of a small stalk. There are many small stalks, all about the same height, and they branch again and again from the main stem, forming a thick cluster. The flowers are very delightful, though they lack the snowy beauty and have none of the delicate scent of the Hawthorn. Each Rowan

PLATE XXVI

THE ROWAN

1. Rowan Tree in Autumn   2. Flower Cluster   3. Leaves and Fruit

PLATE XXVII

THE HAWTHORN

1. Hawthorn Tree in Early Summer   2. Leaves and Blossoms   3. Fruit

flower has five green sepals and five creamy white
petals. These are placed round the end of the
flower stalk, which is slightly swollen, and inside
this swelling lies hidden the seed-vessel; you can
see three sticky threads rising from it in the
centre of the ring of petals. There is a circle of
yellow-headed stamens within the petal ring.

By the end of June the Rowan flowers have faded
and the creamy petals strew the ground. But the
tree does not only depend for its beauty on the
creamy flowers or on the changing leaves.

The swollen flower stalks have been growing
all summer, and now the end of each stalk has
become a small round berry (3), and a dense
cluster of these berries hangs in a bunch from the
main stem. In autumn these berries turn a rich
yellow red, and very brilliant they look among the
dark green leaves. Song birds love these Rowan
berries, and so long as any remain on the tree the
blackbird and thrush will be its constant visitors.

When corn was scarce in the hard winters of
long ago these Rowan berries were dried and
made into flour. Many people to-day make them
into jelly, which is a rich golden colour, but has
rather a bitter taste.

The wood of the Rowan tree is very tough, and
is principally used for making poles.

PLATE XXVII

THE HAWTHORN

" Mark the fair blooming of the Hawthorn tree,
Who, finely clothed in a robe of white,
Fills full the wanton eye with May's delight."

—Chaucer.

We cannot think of the Hawthorn as one of our
noble forest trees, like the Oak and the Beech;
it is dear to us as a village tree, a friendly, bushy
tree which has grown in our garden, or in the
fields and meadows close to our country cottages.
We remember the long sunny May days when we
gathered armfuls of its lovely blossoms, and the
frosty autumn mornings when its berries shone
like rubies on the bare, wind-stripped branches.
It has always been in close touch with our lives,
and it has left many pictures graven deep in our
memory.

The Hawthorn (1), or May, or White-thorn, as
it is often called from the colour of its flowers,
has been known to us since very long ago.
When the hero Ulysses came home from his
weary wanderings, he found his old father
alone; all the servants had gone to the woods
to get young Hawthorn trees to make a hedge,
and the old man was busy digging trenches in
which to plant them.

Even in that far-off time people had discovered
that nothing makes so good a hedge as young

thorn trees. They grow very quickly and send
out many side-shoots and small branches. Each
branch bears sharp thorns, and so closely do
these thorny branches grow together that it is
impossible to push your hand through the hedge
without being badly scratched. Young cattle
and horses love to feed on the Hawthorn leaves,
and one wonders how they can eat them without getting many scatches.

Long after the time of Ulysses we find that
bunches of flowering Hawthorn were carried in
wedding processions as an emblem of hope, and
torches made of its wood were burned. There is
a strange old legend which tells how Joseph of
Arimathea landed on the island of Avalon at
Christmas-tide. He was very weary, and lay
down to rest, but first he planted his staff of
Hawthorn firmly in the ground beside him. And
in the morning he found that the staff had put
out roots and was covered with Hawthorn
blossoms. By this he knew it was meant that
he should stay in Avalon, and he built a monastery
for himself and his brethren and remained there
till he died.

Until not so long ago the country people in
England used to hold gay sports in the village
in the month of May. A tall mast, or Maypole,
was planted in the ground, and the men and
maidens decorated it with wreaths of Hawthorn
blossoms. Then they danced, and sang, and held

merry games around the Maypole in honour of summer's return.

In early spring the Hawthorn tree, if you find one growing singly in a field or meadow, is most easily recognised by its bushy appearance. The tree trunk is dark grey and very rough; often it is twisted like a rope, but it is rarely a thick trunk, as you seldom find a large Hawthorn. Even when very old—about two hundred and fifty years some are said to live—the Hawthorn is always a small tree.

In April the young leaf buds appear; pale green knobs, or little bundles, bursting from every branch. Each leaf (2) is cut up into blunt fingers, and soon it loses its paleness and becomes dark green and glossy. In autumn these leaves change to gold and dark red and brown; but the frosty nights and cold winds soon strip them from the branches.

May is the month when the flowers (2) begin to bloom—clusters of tiny snow-white balls, each at the end of a slender green stalk. In England it was the custom to give a basin of cream for breakfast to the person who first brought home a branch of Hawthorn in blossom on the first of May.

When the flower balls or buds unclose, you find that they have five snow-white petals, which are set in the throat of the calyx cup. Within this ring of petals, round the mouth of the cup, grow many slender stamens, each with a bright pink head. And if you look at the back of the flower, you will see five green points which stand out like the rays of a star behind the white petals. These are the sepals.

Below this green star the stalk looks slightly swollen: this swelling contains the seed, and by the time autumn comes it will have grown into a small green berry. After the white petals and the pink-headed stamens have fallen, you will find clusters of these berries, which are called haws, each with the withered remains of the sepals clinging to the top, as you find them in the Rose and in the Apple. The berries (3) become crimson when the frost comes, and birds eat them greedily.

We have few trees which flower so beautifully as the Hawthorn. In May and June the hedge-rows are laden with its masses of snowy blossoms. Sometimes you will find Hawthorns on which the flowers are a vivid crimson, and these are so transparently beautiful they look as if the light shone through them. And in autumn no tree is more attractive than the Hawthorn, with its gleaming berries and many-coloured leaves.

The wood of the Hawthorn is not very service-able. It is hard and may be highly polished, but the trees are too small for the timber to be useful.

The branches, like those of the Ash and the Whin, burn readily, even when green, and in Scotland the bark was used in olden days to dye wool black.

P

PLATE XXVIII
THE BOX

Many of us only know Box as the name given to the small bushy plant which is placed along the edges of our garden borders to keep the earth from falling out on the gravel path. And we are surprised to learn that this plant is only the Dwarf Box, and that the true Box is a tree, a fair-sized tree, which may be seen any day in Oxford growing to a height of over twenty feet. We must learn to recognise the Box tree, for in the South of England there are still many districts where it grows freely.

It has been known in this country for hundreds of years, but its fame has come down to us in a curious way. In old books we read that the Box was chiefly prized as the tree which would stand more clipping than any other. People in those days had a strange fancy for cutting trees and bushes into quaint shapes. They had Box trees which looked like peacocks, and Box trees shaped like beehives. There were arm-chairs, and tubs, and even statues made of growing Box, cut and trimmed by the gardener's clever shears.

The best gardener then was the one who clipped best, and a very difficult art it was, to clip the tree into a certain shape and yet not to kill it. Nowadays these quaint Box tree curiosities are scarcely ever made, but a Box tree hedge is often planted, and its masses of closely-crowded evergreen leaves afford good protection to young plants in a windy garden.

The Box tree (1) has a dark grey green bark, and the young shoots are four-sided. It grows very slowly—only a few inches each year—and because of this the wood is very hard and fine, as fine as ebony.

The leaves (2) are placed opposite each other, and are small and egg-shaped, with smooth edges. Above they are dark green and very glossy, but underneath the colour is paler. They are very poisonous these Box leaves, and fowls are known to have died from eating them.

The poet Wordsworth tells us that at country funerals it was usual to have a basin filled with sprays of Box standing at the door, and every friend who came to the funeral took a spray, which he carried to the churchyard and laid on the new grave. Rosemary or Yew sprays were often used in the same way.

The flowers are very tiny; you will scarcely be able to see how they are shaped without a magnifying-glass. They grow in crowded yellow clusters at the foot of the leaves, where they join the stem. In each cluster there is usually one seed flower (3) with a tiny green pea in the centre, from which rise three curved horns. All the other flowers will be stamen flowers, which shed plenty of pollen dust over this single green pea. The fruit (4) is a green berry, enclosing a tiny black seed, which you cannot see.

Box-wood is very valuable and is scarce in this country. Most of what we use comes from other lands. In France there is a large Box-wood forest near the village of St. Claude, and all the people in that village spend their days making the Box-wood into small articles, such as forks and spoons, and rosaries and snuff-boxes, for which they get a good deal of money. The wood is pale yellow, and may be cut into the finest pattern without breaking. For many years Box-wood has been used by engravers for making the blocks from which pictures and patterns are printed; the wood is so hard that these blocks can be used many, many times without the edges becoming worn.

Near London there grew a famous wood called Boxhill, and when the trees in that wood were cut down they were sold for ten thousand pounds.

PLATE XXIX

THE WALNUT

The Walnut tree (1) comes to us from sunny Italy and France, where it has grown for many centuries and is greatly prized. Its Latin name, *Juglans*, means the nut of Jove, and the Romans called it

PLATE XXVIII

THE BOX

1. Box Tree   2. Leaf Spray with Flowers   3. Single Flower   4. Fruit

PLATE XXIX

THE WALNUT

1. Walnut Tree 2. Leaf Spray 3. Bud 4. Scar
5. Stamen Flower 6. Seed Flowers 7. Fruit

so because they thought the fruit was worthy to
be set before their chief god Jove. It was brought
to this country about five hundred years ago, and
seems to have been grown in many districts until
the beginning of last century, when there came
a great demand for its wood. As much as six
hundred pounds was given for a single Walnut
tree, and at once all the people who had Walnut
trees cut them down and sold them. This greatly
reduced the number.

It is a large, handsome tree, which grows to a
considerable height, and has a very thick trunk
covered with grey bark. This trunk is smooth
when the tree is young, but turns rugged as it
grows older. The Walnut branches are large
and spreading; they are sometimes twisted, but
the tips of each branch always turn to the sky.
For long it was thought to be dangerous to sleep
beneath the shade of a Walnut tree, but for what
reason I have not been able to discover.

The leaves (2) are very handsome; each leaf is
made up of several pairs of leaflets placed opposite
each other on a central stalk, with a single leaflet at the end. When they first come out these
leaflets are dull red, but the colour soon changes
to a pale olive green, and each leaf is smooth and
soft and has a delicious scent if crushed ever so
slightly. The twigs which carry these leaves are
very stout, even to the tips, but they break easily,
and you will find many lying on the ground after

a windy night. The bark on these young twigs is very smooth and glossy.

The Walnut tree produces two kinds of flowers, which are both found on the same tree, and one kind, the stamen flowers (5), requires a whole year to ripen. If you look at the twigs which support the leaves you will see several tiny cone-shaped buds (3) dotted here and there on either side, close to the scars (4) left by last year's leaf stalk. These are the beginnings of next year's stamen flowers, and they remain like that all summer and all winter until the following spring. Then the bud lengthens and becomes a slender, drooping catkin (5). This catkin is covered with small flowers, each made up of five green sepals enclosing many stamens. These stamen catkins drop from the tree when the pollen dust is scattered.

The Walnut seed flowers (6) are so small that they require to be looked for carefully. They grow among the leaves at the end of the twig, and their small seed-vessels, each with a closely-fitting calyx covering, are ready before the leaves come out. Very soon the small seeds develop into smooth green fruits, which continue to grow all summer, and in July they are the size of a small plum. This fruit is a nut (7), the famous Walnut, and at first you will not see in it any likeness to the Walnut which we eat at dessert after cracking the pale brown shell. But look more closely. The green fruit is a soft juicy envelope which conceals a large nut. This green envelope turns brown when it is ripe and splits open, showing the nut inside, a nut with a crinkled skin, which is soft and green at first, but which becomes a hard, pale brown shell when the fruit dries. It is the kernel of this nut which we eat with salt as a dessert fruit.

The Walnuts usually ripen in October, but often they are gathered in July before the juicy green covering has turned brown, and they are preserved in vinegar and used as a pickle. Ripe Walnuts contain a great deal of oil, and the oil is much valued by artists, who mix it with their paints. It is the most liquid of all the oils, and it dries very quickly.

If you look at your fingers after gathering Walnuts you will find that they are stained a dark brown. The Walnut tree contains a juice which leaves a dark stain. It is said that with this juice the gipsies dye their skin brown; and it is also used to stain floors.

Walnut wood is very valuable. It is light in weight and dark in colour, with beautiful veins and streaks throughout. Much fine furniture is made of Walnut wood, and it can be polished till it shines like satin. To-day it is largely used in the manufacture of guns and rifles.

You will now understand what an important tree the Walnut is, as it yields fruit and oil and wood, which are all valuable.

PLATE XXX

THE SWEET CHESTNUT OR SPANISH CHESTNUT

The Sweet Chestnut is a cousin of the Oak, and belongs with it to the great family of cup-bearing trees, or those that bear their fruit sitting in a cup. Like the Oak, it is a tree with a great and ancient history, although nowadays we are apt to take little notice of this tree, which was once well known and grew abundantly in many parts of England.

The largest Chestnut in the world grows in Sicily, in the great forest which covers the slopes of Mount Etna. It is said that a Spanish Queen was once overtaken in this forest by a tremendous storm, and that she and a hundred soldiers and horses were all able to find shelter beneath the wide-spreading branches of this one tree.

In this country we have a famous big Chestnut tree in Gloucestershire which is believed to be a thousand years old; it is written about in old books, which tell us that this tree belonged to a certain house in the time of King Stephen.

The Sweet Chestnut (1) is a large bushy tree with beautiful leaves, which painters love to put in the background of their pictures. The branches are heavy and spreading, and they sweep downwards. Each branch is thickly covered with long green leaves (2), which are so thick and glossy

that you expect them to be evergreen. Each leaf
is sharply oval, and has a stout rib running up
the centre, from which straight veins branch to
the very edge of the leaf, where they each end in a
point. These points make the edge of the leaf look
as if toothed. Insects do not destroy these Chestnut leaves, and they hang on the twigs till late in
autumn, when they turn pale yellow; this yellow
deepens to gold and brown, and when winter
comes they cover the ground with a thick carpet
of rustling leaves. These leaves are often gathered
to make winter bedding for the poor people, who
call them "talking beds" because they rustle and
crackle so when lain on.

Those leaves that are left on the ground greatly
enrich the soil.

The trunk of the Chestnut tree is scored up and
down with many deep ridges, and these ridges
seem to bend round the tree strangely, as if they
had been twisted, like the strands of a rope, when
the tree was young and tender.

The Chestnut flowers appear on this year's
shoots early in May or June, and they are of two
kinds, both of which grow on the same tree.
The stamen flowers (3) are in long catkin spikes,
which rise stiffly among the leaves. The centre
stem of the catkin is very stout, and seated round
it are tufts of yellow-headed stamens, each enclosed
in a green calyx. These stamen heads are filled
with yellow dust, which they shed in the same way

Q

as the Pine tree stamens, in such quantities that it lies like sulphur on any still lake or pond that may be near.

On the same catkin spike, near the foot, grow the seed-flowers (4). These look like short, fat paint brushes with a stout green handle. There is a cup made up of many slender green leaf-like points, and inside this cup sit the seeds; you can see a bunch of their points standing up like the bristles of the paint brush. When plenty of the stamen dust has fallen on these bristles, the seed sets about getting ready its fruit, and the stamen part of the catkin spike shrivels and falls off; its work is done.

But the seed grows bigger and bigger, till it looks like a round green ball (5) covered all over with bristles. The seeds are ripening inside this ball, two or three, sometimes five, seeds closely packed side by side. In October the green covering splits into four pieces and the seeds fall to the ground. Notice how beautifully this bristly covering is lined with soft, silky down to protect the smooth skin of the nut.

Each nut is slightly flattened at the sides where it was tightly pressed against its neighbour, and it comes to a point at the top, where the withered remains of the seed bristles show in a dry brown tuft. The skin on the Chestnut is dark brown, and there is a large scar at the foot of the nut where it was fastened to the green cup.

In Italy, where there are miles and miles of Chestnut forests, the nuts are gathered in sackfuls when October comes. They are then spread out on a brick floor in a thick layer, and a fire, made of dry leaves and sticks, is lit beneath. This fire is kept burning for ten days, and the nuts are frequently turned with a wooden shovel. Whenever the skins crack off quite easily the nuts are ready; the hard, cracked brown skins are removed, and the nuts are ground into flour from which many delicious foods are prepared.

The fruit of the Chestnut is one of the most important tree fruits we know. In France and Italy the people use Chestnuts as much as we do potatoes, and many are the clever ways in which they prepare and cook them, but the commonest way is to boil and eat the chestnuts with a little salt. When the cook is preparing the nuts, he makes a slit in the skin of every Chestnut except one, and when that one bursts and cracks with a loud noise, he knows that the others are ready.

The Chestnut fruit ripens in the South of England, but it is never so large, nor is it so plentiful, as in the sunny South.

The wood of the Chestnut tree is valuable. For many years people believed that the great beams in some of our old historic buildings were Chestnut wood, and this made them think that the trees must have grown much larger then than

they do to-day. But it is now decided that these
old beams must be made of Oak. Old Oak beams
are very like Chestnut beams, but clever people
tell us that Chestnut wood is best when it is
young, as the old wood is apt to break off in
little pieces, and it would not really be a suitable
wood to use in buildings where strength was
needed.

Chestnut wood makes excellent fences and
is also used for wine casks; the hoops which
go round these wine casks should be made of
it, as it does not rot in a damp cellar. Chestnut
wood burns badly; it sends up a great many
sparks, and it smoulders, but will not burn
brightly.

PLATE XXXI

THE HORSE CHESTNUT

The Horse Chestnut is not related in any way
to the Sweet Chestnut; there is no resemblance
between them except the appearance of their nuts,
and even in these there are many points of difference. It is said that the name Horse Chestnut
was given because the nuts of this tree were
only fit for horses to eat, whereas the Sweet
Chestnuts are valuable as a food for human beings.
Even horses will not eat the nuts of the Horse
Chestnut tree. You must not forget that if the

PLATE XXX

THE SWEET CHESTNUT

1. Sweet Chestnut Tree   2. Leaf Spray with Flowers   3. Stamen Flowers
4. Seed Flowers   5. Fruit in Case

PLATE XXXI

THE HORSE CHESTNUT

1. Horse Chestnut Tree in Autumn   2. Young Leaf   3. Full-grown Leaf
4. Sticky Bud in Leaf Scar   5. Flower Spike   6. Single Flower
7. Fruit in Case

Chestnut is spoken of without an adjective, it is the sweet Spanish Chestnut that has the right to the name, and is by far the more valuable tree.

The Horse Chestnut (1) was brought to this country five hundred years ago, and we prize it greatly for its beautiful flowers and leaves. It has a large, stout trunk, covered with a rough, scaly bark, on which you will frequently notice many green patches caused by a tiny plant which makes its home there.

The branches are large and spreading, and they sweep downwards to the ground, then rise again towards the tips, forming graceful curves. The shoots bearing the buds always point towards the sky, and in spring these shoots grow very fast for about a month, then they do not become any larger, but the shoot thickens and is soon tough and woody.

All winter the Horse Chestnut buds can be seen on the tree—large, dark, purply brown buds (4) covered with a thick coating of sticky gum. In April these buds begin to swell and the gummy covering melts. It held together twelve dark brown scales, and these fall to the ground, showing an under layer of paler scales. The growing bud inside soon pushes itself through these scales, and the young leaf appears, a delicate, pale green bud, with its leaves closely folded like a fan. They open very quickly in the warm sunshine, but for some days after they have shaken themselves loose from the scaly coverings each leaf (2) hangs on its stalk like a half-opened parasol, with all its tips pointing to the ground. But soon the leaf tips rise, and the parasol is fully opened and a beautiful leafy screen it is.

The leaf (3) is cut up into seven leaflets, and every leaflet is shaped like a pear, with the broad part pointing outwards and the narrow end joining the leaf stalk. These pear-shaped leaflets are not all the same size; there are two which are quite small and two a little larger, and the other three are larger still. The leaflets have small teeth round their edges, and there is a raised rib running up the centre, from which branches a network of fine veins all over the leaflet.

The Horse Chestnut leaves grow opposite each other in pairs, and each pair is placed cross-ways to the pair farther down on the branch, in the same way as those of the Sycamore. In July the leaves begin to change colour; they turn red and brown, and they fall very early in autumn. Look closely at the twigs and you will see on them many curious marks shaped like horse-shoes; these are the scars (4) where a leaf stalk joined the twig, and above each of these scars you can see next year's leaf bud already distinctly formed.

In May the Horse Chestnut is in flower (5), and a wonderful sight it is; the tree is laden with snowy spikes, which look like great candles set on a bushy Christmas tree. A giant's nosegay, it is sometimes called by the country people, this great tree, with its wealth of fan-shaped leaves and these stiff snow-white spikes rising from every branch.

The lowest flowers (6) in each spike open first, and they are called by botanists perfect flowers, because each one has all its parts complete. They have a green bell-shaped calyx with five divisions round the mouth. Within this calyx are five separate white petals, one of which is much larger than the others, and these petals have many hairs on them and are splashed with crimson and yellow stains.

In the throat of this flower there are seven stamens with curved stalks and pale salmon-coloured heads, and among these you can see a slender curved green thread rising from the seed-vessel, which lies hidden in the centre of the flower.

The upper flowers on the spike have no seed-vessel, and they fall off as soon as their stamen dust is scattered. The spike may bear thirty or forty flowers, yet only a few will remain to produce seeds after the beautiful petals are withered.

When this has happened the seed-vessel grows larger and larger till it becomes a rough, horny green ball (7) studded with short spines. It is not bristly all over like the Sweet Chestnut fruit ball, but is hard and smooth, and its spines are thick and clumsy, with a wide space between each. If you open one of these balls before the fruit is ripe, you will find a nut inside, which is white and polished like a piece of ivory and which fits the covering closely. But if you leave the fruit to ripen on the tree, then the green ball splits into three pieces, and you see that the nut (7) inside has shrunk a little and has become a rich, dark brown. It is so glossy that it looks as if it had just been oiled, and it is almost round.

There is a white scar at the foot of the nut, where it was fastened to the inside of the green ball.

In the Sweet Chestnut, you remember, there were always two or three nuts inside each bristly ball, and these nuts were dull, and not glossy like those of the Horse Chestnut.

Although horses will not eat this fruit, deer and cattle and sheep all like it. In this country the nuts are usually left to rot on the ground where they fall. After they decay these nuts may be pounded and made into a kind of soap; they contain a juice which is said to be good for cleansing.

The Horse Chestnut is a very fast-growing tree. In fourteen years a tree grown from a nut will be large enough to sit under, and the wood, on this account, is less hard and lasting than woods that have taken longer to grow. It is used for cabinet-making and for flooring.

The tree does not produce any fruit till it is

PLATE XXXII

THE CEDAR

1. Cedar Tree   2. Leaf Spray   3. Stamen Flower

4. Seed Flower   5. Closed Cone and Open Cone

twenty years old, but after that it will bear nuts yearly till it is two hundred.

There is a variety of Horse Chestnut with pink flowers, which has not been so long known as the white-flowered tree.

PLATE XXXII

THE CEDAR OF LEBANON

In the Old Testament we read that when Solomon was building the temple he sent to Hiram, King of Tyre, for stores of goodly Cedar wood from the forests of Lebanon. And Hiram sent the wood by sea in floats, or rafts, as much Cedar and timber of Fir as King Solomon wanted. This was used to cover the stonework of the temple, within and without.

There is a delightful fragrance in these planks of Cedar wood which is said to come from the sap or resin with which the tree abounds. Cedar oil is made from this resin, and it was long in use as a safeguard against the attacks of insects, which dislike the smell.

The Cedar (1), as we see it in this country, rarely rises to the dignity of a large tree; it is most familiar to us as a stunted, bushy tree with a thick, short trunk divided into more than one main stem. Short branches rise from these stems, and at first these point upwards to the sky, but after the branch has grown some length it bends

R

backward and stands straight out from the tree. From a distance the tree looks as if the branches grew in layers, or shelves, with a clear space between each shelf. You will always recognise a Cedar by these layers of branches densely covered with gloomy green leaves. It is said that in countries where much snow falls the Cedar branches always remain upright, because the tree knows that it could not carry the great weight of snow that would gather on its leafy shelves if they grew flat as in warmer lands.

The Cedar is frequently found growing in churchyards, beside the Yew tree, and a dark, gloomy tree it is. The trunk is covered with a thick rough bark of a pale greenish brown colour, but on the branches this bark is thin and flaky. The Cedar grows very slowly. The tree may be a hundred years old before it produces any seeds, though you sometimes find seedless cones on Cedars that are twenty-five to thirty years old.

The leaves (2) are evergreen, and usually remain on the twigs for four or five years. They grow in tufts, like those of the Larch, on the upper side of the twig; but each leaf is needle-shaped, as in the Scotch Pine, and is much harder than the soft Larch leaves. In colour they are a dark bluey green.

The Cedar has two kinds of flowers. Those that bear the stamens (3) appear at the end of short, stunted little twigs which have taken many years to grow. The stamens are in slender catkins, about two inches long, and are a pale reddish yellow colour.

The seed flowers (4) grow in cones, and the Cedar of Lebanon has very curious cones. They grow in pairs, and are like fat green eggs, sitting upright on the branch, with the blunt end uppermost. These cones look quite solid, because the scales are so tightly pressed together. You can scarcely see where one begins and the other ends. It takes two or three years before these scales unclose, and during that time the cones (5) become a rich, dark purple. When the scales unclose, the three-cornered seeds are blown out by the wind, and each seed is furnished with a wing to float it away on the air. The Cedar cones remain on the tree several years after all their seeds have fallen.

The timber of the Cedars grown in this country is of little value; the tree is usually planted for ornament. But in warmer lands, where there are large forests of mighty Cedar trees, the wood is sold for a great deal of money.

PRINTED IN GREAT BRITAIN AT
THE PRESS OF THE PUBLISHERS